MW00986929

CHRISTIANITY AND
AUTOSUGGESTION

CHRISTIANITY AND AUTOSUGGESTION

BY

C. HARRY BROOKS
Author of " The Practice of Autosuggestion "

AND THE

Rev. ERNEST CHARLES

So every spirit, as it is most pure,
And hath in it the more of heavenly light,
So it the fairer bodie doth procure
To habit in, and is more fairely dight
With chearefull grace and amiable sight;
For of the soule the bodie forme doth take;
For soule is forme, and doth the bodie make.
Spenser: *An Hymn in Honour of Beautie*

NEW YORK
DODD, MEAD AND COMPANY
1923

COPYRIGHT, 1923,
BY DODD, MEAD AND COMPANY, INC.

PRINTED IN THE U. S. A. BY
The Quinn & Boden Company
BOOK MANUFACTURERS
RAHWAY   NEW JERSEY

TO THE CHRISTIANS OF ALL
CHURCHES—AND OF NONE

PREFACE

THE distinctive feature of M. Coué's method, compared with other popular methods of self-healing, lies in the fact that it reposes on purely psychological bases. This is its value. We may be reproached with robbing it, in this book, of its psychological foundation and confusing its clarity with mystical speculation. But this is not so. The value of M. Coué's psychological doctrine and of his technical method is in no sense denied or depreciated in these pages. We compare and contrast his teaching with the teaching of Christ on cognate subjects. Finding between them an essential harmony, we attempt to place autosuggestion in its true position in Christian life and thought, and to utilise the Christian dynamic for extending and deepening its power. The secular practice of autosuggestion continues unaltered, but side by side with it we attempt to erect, in essential outlines, a Christian practice of autosuggestion.

Owing to limitations of space, we have been compelled to assume in the reader an elementary knowledge of M. Coué's work. To those who are unacquainted with the subject we would recommend a preliminary reading of *The Practice of Autosuggestion*,[1] which could be followed up with M. Coué's booklet *Self*

[1] *The Practice of Autosuggestion*, by C. Harry Brooks. (Dodd, Mead and Company.)

8   CHRISTIANITY AND AUTOSUGGESTION

Mastery and Professor Baudouin's classic treatise *Suggestion and Autosuggestion.*[1]

From the religious viewpoint our subject is admirably touched on by Dr. R. F. Horton in his new book, *The Mystical Quest of Christ,* and in the following works: *The Life of the Spirit and the Life of To-day,* by Evelyn Underhill; *Autosuggestion and Religion,* by H. C. Carter, M.A.; *Religion and Medicine,* by Worcester and McComb; *The Christian Religion as a Healing Power,* by the same authors; *Spiritual and Mental Healing,* by E. M. Caillard; *Miracles and the New Psychology,* by E. R. Micklem, M.A.; *Psychology and the Christian Life,* by T. W. Pym, M.A., and *M. Coué and His Gospel of Health,* by the Dean of Chester.

We have naturally been obliged to discuss in these pages some of the great themes of theology, but we have done so only when the orientation of our subject demanded it, and, we trust, in a simple and straightforward manner. We hope that where the views advanced here do not find acceptance they will at least furnish food for thought and aid in the furtherance of truth.

We have tried as far as possible to indicate our indebtedness to other writers. If there are any omissions, they are unintentional, and will, we feel sure, be forgiven.

C. H. B.
E. C.

MALVERN LINK,
  February 21, 1923.

[1] Published by Dodd, Mead and Company.

CONTENTS

9

PART II

CHRISTIAN AUTOSUGGESTION

CONTENTS   13

PART I

AUTOSUGGESTION AND THE
  TEACHING OF CHRIST

CHAPTER I

INTRODUCTORY

"If I only knew that God was as good as that woman, I should be content."

"Then you don't believe that God is good?"

"I didn't say that, my boy. But to know that God was good and kind and fair—heartily, I mean, and not half-ways with ifs and buts. My boy, there would be nothing left to be miserable about."

GEORGE MACDONALD: *Robert Falconer.*

WITHIN the last few years psychological science has invaded those regions of the soul where hitherto religion has held undisputed sway. In this intrusion Autosuggestion may be said to penetrate further than the complementary method of Psychoanalysis, for while the latter, by removing inhibitions, seeks to restore a man to his normal self, autosuggestion undertakes, by developing his mental and moral potentialities, to make him more than his normal self, to make a nobler and better man of him. This, of course, is the Christian aim.

Thus autosuggestion, working along a purely psychological channel, seems to set itself up in rivalry with Christianity, to be a new religion, though without a God. Many Christians feel—and their feeling is worthy of all respect—that they " cannot play tricks with their souls." M. Coué requires them to repeat morning and night a formula which assures them that in every way they are growing better and better, and they cannot forbear from asking to Whom or to What this formula is addressed. With a personal conviction of the nearness of Christ they hesitate to bow down, like the men of Athens, before an Unknown God. This was the attitude taken up by Dean Inge on M. Coué's arrival in England in March 1922, though, we believe, his views have since become much more favourable to the moral value of M. Coué's teaching.

But there are other Christians who feel no such scruples. Autosuggestion appears to them to offer a valuable means of achieving in fuller measure the ideals set before them by Jesus Christ. They introduce the name of God into their daily formula and ascribe the benefits which result from it to His beneficent care. The Bishop of Manchester in *The Pilgrim* (October 1922) finds one aspect of M. Coué's teaching to agree substantially with that of St. Paul, and Dr. R. F. Horton claims that the discovery of the Law of Reversed Effort " opens an immense unexplored field of religious development." Whichever view we may take, it must be admitted that the relation of Christianity to autosuggestion calls imperatively for attention.

It is interesting to note that those people who have come into the most intimate contact with M. Coué are under no doubts as to the moral value of the method he advocates. They find it to be consonant with the teaching of Christ and effective as a means of practising that love towards one's neighbour which is one form of love towards God. " The more I study autosuggestion," writes a lady of Nancy, " the better I understand the divine law of confidence and love given to us by Christ. ' Thou shalt love thy neighbour,' and by giving him a little of your heart and of your moral force, help him to rise if he is fallen and to cure himself if he is sick." Indeed, M. Coué himself, though keeping his religious views very much in the background, lives a life in which the practical virtues of Christianity are clearly manifest. "He is a power of goodness," says Mme. Emile Léon, one of his nearest associates, "indefatigably painstaking, active and smiling, ready to help every one." While Mr. Hugh MacNaghten writes as follows: "M. Coué seems to have divined from the first that loving is its own reward. Rich and poor, bad and good, to him they are all men and women, and if they need his help he gives it to them, without distinction, in his all-embracing charity." [1]

These personal considerations are not without their own value. They are quoted to show that, if one may judge from the unsought opinions of those most nearly concerned, there is nothing in M. Coué or his methods which is inimical to practical Christianity. But there is one point of agreement which is surely self-evident. M. Coué's method stands on a foundation of profound optimism. To believe that day by day, in every way, we are getting better and better, is to believe, at least implicitly, that the Power at the heart of the universe is friendly to humanity, that, however the actual life of man may fall short of perfection, the Source is benignant and pure. Indeed, the faith behind this formula goes further still. It implies that a channel exists in us by which this ultimate strength and goodness may be made active in our daily life; it assumes that the machinery of the mind is so constructed as to give to this beneficent Power a more direct way of expression than we have commonly supposed.

Surely this is the basis of Christ's own teaching. He

---

[1] *Emile Coué, the Man and his Work*, p. 47.

taught us that God is our Father, that His nature is essentially love, and that we need but call upon His aid and it will be given to us. If there be Christians who refuse to accept this as God's essential nature, we can only conclude that they cherish a conception of God at variance with that held by their Master. If they prefer to think of God as hostile to man, vindictive, resentful, capricious in affection, only answering prayer at the last extremity and after passionate appeals; if, in short, they regard God, though perhaps not consciously, as " the tyrant of the world," then they had better lay this book aside; M. Coué has no message for them;—but then neither has Christ.

CHAPTER II

CHRIST, THE HEALER

I went to a meeting at Arne-side, where Richard Myer was, who had been long lame of one of his arms. I was moved of the Lord to say unto him, among all the people, " Stand up on thy legs " : and he stood up and stretched out his arm and said, " Be it known unto you, all people, that this day I am healed." Yet his parents could hardly believe it; and they took him aside, took off his doublet, and then saw that it was true.

Fox's Journal (1653).

FEW intelligent persons would attempt at the present day to throw doubt on the veracity of Christ's miracles of healing. The scepticism which regarded them as a transgression of natural law and therefore set them down as mere legends, sprang from a premature judgment based on insufficient knowledge. Modern psychotherapeutics tends increasingly to show that, in His works of healing, Christ was not transgressing the laws of Nature, but utilising laws of which science is just becoming dimly aware. Indeed, the wonder would have been if Christ had failed to heal—when Quimby and the Christian Scientists succeed! It would be incredible if no mighty works had attended the passage of this Divine Figure across the stage of human life.

It is obvious that Christ was essentially a mental healer. He made no use of drugs, of massage, or of manipulative surgery. It is true that he smeared the eyes of a blind man with clay and ordered him to wash in a pool. But clay is no specific against blindness, and the waters of Siloam had no intrinsic healing virtue. These physical means had a purely psychological value.

Christ's cures were mind cures. Christ was, then, not only the Great Physician, He was also the Great Psychologist.

If we would grasp the meaning of His " psychological " teaching it must be in the same way as we grasp any other intellectual truth—by analysis. It is possible to abstract from Christ's whole teaching one element— the psychological and therapeutic, and having done so we are justified in comparing and contrasting this isolated segment with the purely scientific theories which are being formulated to-day. Such is the intention of this little book.

Whatever M. Coué's virtues may be, it would be an offence against common sense, a denial of any sane standard of values, to think of setting him on so sublime a height as to compare him with our Lord. He is the inventor of a technical method by which the power of autosuggestion, which we all possess, can be applied to healing. Christ is our Divine Master. It must be clearly recognised that the comparisons which occur in the following pages are between M. Coué's theories and one limited aspect of our Lord's teaching, viz., that which is concerned with the working of the mind. There is nowhere any intention of effecting a comparison between the two personalities. On this clear understanding we can proceed to compare different aspects of Christ's healing with that performed by contemporary methods of autosuggestion.

" When a paralytic is cured on the spot, when he rushes to the window of the little upper room in Nancy, when he shouts to the people who are gathering for the next *conférence* in the courtyard below, ' *Je marche, je marche,*' our thoughts go back nearly two thousand years to the beautiful gate of the Temple, where a certain man, lame from his mother's womb, at Peter's word, leaping up, ' stood and walked and entered with them into the Temple, walking and leaping and praising God.' "

Thus Mr. Hugh MacNaghten [1] records his own experience, and apparently that of his companions, on witnessing M. Coué at work in his Nancy clinic. And some such thoughts inevitably occur to the mind of any visitor who is familiar, even to a slight extent, with the records of the life of Jesus. One is conscious of a sense of active benevolence, emanating not only from the practitioner, but from the crowd of sufferers, a feeling of complete and cheerful goodwill, as if the coldnesses, the suspicions, the criticisms and hostilities so prevalent in the outside world had been sloughed off at the entrance to this simple little room; as if, with faith, love too had entered.

This similarity of atmosphere is interesting, though in no sense conclusive. We note it in passing because it has been felt by many independent observers.

But apart from superficial resemblances we must try to discover whether there is in the method used by M. Coué any similarity with the method used by our Lord. The New Testament, of course, gives us no detailed medical diagnoses of the disorders cured by Jesus. Indications of the nature of the complaint are always vague. But we must admit that our Lord's method did not involve the careful diagnosis required by modern physical methods of healing. His method was substantially the same, *whatever* the nature of the disease. This unique quality it also shares with the method of autosuggestion. M. Coué has frequently been blamed by medical men for what is regarded as

[1] Op. cit., p. 39.

his slipshod neglect of this primary factor in medical treatment. His critics do not realise that his method is substantially the same *whatever* the nature of the disease, that it works by setting right those profound sources of life to which health in every part of our organism is due. Diagnosis is left to the doctors whose physical aid M. Coué gladly welcomes. For his specific work, diagnosis, at least if its conclusions were communicated to the patient, would be a hindrance rather than a help. In the quotations which follow, both when they refer to our Lord's healing and to the work done in Nancy, we must be content to forego diagnostic exactitude.

"*And it came to pass also on another sabbath, that he entered into the synagogue and taught: and there was a man whose right hand was withered. And the scribes and Pharisees watched him, whether he would heal on the sabbath day; that they might find an accusation against him. But he knew their thoughts, and said to the man which had his hand withered, Rise up, and stand forth in the midst. And he arose and stood forth. And Jesus said unto them, I ask you, Is it lawful on the sabbath to do good, or to do harm, to save life or to destroy it? And he looked round about on them all, and said unto him, Stretch forth thy hand. And he did so: and his hand was restored.*" [1]

" ' Now, listen,' said Coué. ' For ten years you have been thinking you could not lift your hand above your shoulder; consequently you have not been able to do so, for whatever we think becomes true for us. Now think, I can lift it.'

" The patient looked at him doubtfully.

[1] St. Luke vi. 6-10.

" 'Quick!' Coué said in a tone of authority. 'Think, I can, I can.'

" 'I can,' said the man. He made a half-hearted attempt, and complained of a pain in his shoulder.

" '*Bon*,' said Coué. 'Don't lower your arm. Close your eyes and repeat with me as fast as you can, *ça passe, ça passe.*'

" For half a minute they repeated this phrase together, speaking so fast as to produce a sound like the whirl of a rapidly revolving machine. Meanwhile Coué quickly stroked the man's shoulder. At the end of that time the patient admitted that his pain had left him.

" ' Now think well that you can lift your arm,' Coué said.

" The departure of the pain had given the patient faith. His face, which before had been perplexed and incredulous, brightened as the thought of power took possession of him. ' I can,' he said in a tone of finality, and without effort he calmly lifted his arm to its full height above his head. He held it there triumphantly for a moment while the whole company applauded and encouraged him.

"Coué reached for his hand and shook it.

" ' My friend, you are cured.' " [1]

In the passage quoted from St. Luke there are two motifs: Christ's conflict with the scribes and Pharisees over the legality of healing on the Sabbath, and that immediately interesting to us—the actual healing. Comparing the latter with the instance quoted from

---

[1] *Practice of Autosuggestion*, chap. i. (NOTE.—I must apologise for quoting my own book, but so far as I know it is the only one which gives a detailed descriptive account of M. Coué's work in Nancy. C.H.B.)

M. Coué's practice we find similarities and differences which are equally instructive. The patients were suffering from similar disorders: a withered hand and a paralysed arm. Both were cured by purely mental means without the introduction of any material aid. In each case the spoken word was the instrument of cure. Christ's action on this occasion divides itself into three stages: (1) He commanded the sufferer to stand forth. (2) He kept him standing for an appreciable time, while He discussed with the onlookers the question of healing on the Sabbath. (3) He commanded the man to perform an action which proved that his withered member was already restored.

The *modus operandi* of M. Coué's healing presents striking similarities with the above. It may be analysed as follows: (1) An explanation of the principles of healing by autosuggestion. (2) An experiment to prove their veracity (neither of these occur in our quotation). (3) A command that the man should perform the action by thinking he can do so. (4) The removal of pain. (5) The successful performance of the action. Let us try to realise the psychological processes through which the mind of each patient had to pass. In each case we may assume that the sufferer desired to be healed and possessed a certain degree of faith in his healer. It was expected that Christ would heal in the synagogue, for we are told " the scribes and Pharisees watched him whether he would heal," and it is quite probable that the man with the withered hand had come with the express purpose of invoking Christ's aid; a similar intention, of course, had brought the paralytic to M. Coué's clinic. What were the thoughts of the man with the withered hand on being commanded by Jesus to stand forth in the midst? He was aware of Christ's previous miracles, and would undoubtedly assume that he himself was about to be healed. Listening anxiously to the words addressed to the Pharisees he found that our Lord took for granted His power to heal and that His opponents did not dare to challenge it. The only doubt was whether our Lord would heal on the Sabbath or would postpone the healing till a later day. In the sufferer's anxiety whether Jesus would *consent* to heal him the belief is implied that our Lord *could* heal him. Thus as he stood listening his faith was subtly raised to the point of action. " Stretch forth thy hand," said Christ, and without questioning his ability he obeyed.[1]

M. Coué's patient also passed by gradual steps from a vague hope of cure to complete certainty. In the earlier stages of the sitting the patient heard the evidence of those already helped by the use of autosuggestion; he listened to a simple but convincing proof of its reasonableness; he discovered by experiment that it applied to him, and was led to see that his disability would be removed as soon as the right thought took possession of his mind. During this process his faith was gradually strengthening, his expectancy growing more intense. But it had not yet reached action-point: he faltered at the command to lift his arm. Only the relief of the pain overcame the last doubt and completed his cure. We see that the states of mind the patient passed through were similar in both cases. But

[1] As Mr. Pym says (*Psychology and the Christian Life,* p. 107) : " The argument of Jesus has a double point; apparently He is teaching what we now call the Christian view of Sunday observance; in effect He was also turning the cripple's hope into absolute conviction. Here was a healer apparently not concerned as to whether he, the patient, *could* be cured, but merely arguing in favour of curing him to-day rather than to-morrow ! "

we are dealing with mind-cures in which these mental states are of capital importance. We may say that the man with the withered hand and the paralysed blacksmith both underwent a process which aroused in them an absolute certainty that they were going to be cured.

The differences between the two cases are also worth noting. Though M. Coué's cure was an unusually rapid one, it was slow and laborious compared with that of our Lord. It contained a greater number of steps, and did not exhibit the same psychological subtlety or the same completely sure touch. No doubt it is probable, as Mr. Micklem points out,[1] that the Gospel account may mislead us into thinking that our Lord's healing was more rapid than it actually was; the conversation between Christ and the Pharisees, for instance, was probably longer than is reported. Nevertheless, even allowing for this, Christ cured more radically and more rapidly than M. Coué.

It would be tedious to quote other cases, and in view of the considerations which follow it is hardly necessary. We have recognised that the process by which Jesus healed the man of his withered hand was at least *accompanied* by a gradual heightening of the man's expectancy of cure; while in M. Coué's case a somewhat laborious technique was employed with the same end in view—the production of confident and intense expectancy. Now this confident expectancy is frequently called in popular language, *faith*. And if we look through the records of the life of Jesus we find that this word " faith " was continually upon His lips. He taught that faith was an absolute necessity to life, that with faith His disciples could do works as mighty

[1] *Miracles and the New Psychology*, p. 131.

as His own, while without faith they were powerless.

We must try to ascertain what Jesus meant by faith and what was the relation of this faith to the confident expectancy which is the means of healing employed in autosuggestion.

CHAPTER III

WHAT IS FAITH?

It is an affirmation and an act
That bids eternal truth be present fact.
HARTLEY COLERIDGE.

THE word faith is frequently used to indicate intellectual belief. We speak of the Christian faith, and by that we mean a vaguely defined body of dogma to which, it is assumed, the orthodox Christian subscribes. This is the significance which many people give to the word in reading the New Testament. But we must doubt whether they are justified in doing so. It will be well to consider a few of the instances in which faith is spoken of by Jesus.

" The blind men came to him: and Jesus saith unto them, Believe ye that I am able to do this? They say unto him, Yea, Lord. Then touched he their eyes, saying, According to your faith be it done unto you. And their eyes were opened." [1]

Our Lord asks the sufferers in the simplest terms if they believe He can cure them, and when they answer affirmatively He ascribes their healing to their faith, i.e., to the belief that they were about to be healed. To contend that by faith Christ means in this instance the acceptance of His theological teaching or a belief in His divinity is quite indefensibly to pervert His meaning.

It may, however, be contended that Christ's question

[1] St. Matt. ix. 28-29.

was equivalent to this: "Do you believe that I am the Son of God and in virtue of My divine sonship have power to heal you?" Thus the expectancy of cure would be made contingent upon the acknowledgment of Christ's divinity. And this may actually have been the case. But if so we must distinguish in the effective faith two elements: (1) The acknowledgment of Christ's divine nature; and (2) the expectancy of cure to which this belief gave rise. Which of these two was the healing factor?

The devout Christian will be tempted, perhaps, to choose the former. But is the evidence with him? If a belief in the divinity of the healer was an essential condition of cure then none but a divine personality— or a charlatan, who falsely inspired this belief—could heal. How comes it, then, that the disciples possessed this gift? They were not gods, but neither were they tricksters. "And the seventy returned with joy, saying, Lord, even the demons are subject unto us in Thy name." [1]

One may object that the disciples were able to heal because Christ had personally conferred upon them the powers proper to Himself. But if so we have to explain the fact that an unauthorised person, of whom apparently Christ had never heard, was found by the disciples "casting out demons." Surely it is too much to claim that this unknown man was in some mysterious way the recipient of Christ's personal and unique gifts. The disciples, very humanly, objected to this infringement of their rights. They were inclined, as we are inclined, to regard healing as a power appertaining only to Christ and to those whom He author-

[1] St. Luke x. 17.

ised. Therefore they forbade him "because he followed not us." We find, however, that Jesus was not in agreement with them. He rebuked them for their hasty and unauthorised action, saying: "Forbid him not." [1]

This leads us to the conclusion that the faith by which men were healed did not necessarily involve an acknowledgment of Christ's divinity on the part of the sufferer, that, in fact, the deciding factor was a simple expectancy of cure. [2] We cannot examine here more than one or two relevant examples, but it is very essential to see whether this hypothesis can maintain itself.

No miracle of healing is reported with so much circumstantial detail as that in John ix. Jesus encounters a man blind from his birth. He moistens the dust with saliva, anoints the man's eyes with the clay and orders him to wash in the Pool of Siloam. The man obeys Him and returns with his sight restored. To his neighbours who ask the identity of his healer, he replies: " A man that is called Jesus." The Pharisees arrive, incensed that this work of healing should have been performed on the Sabbath, and there is a difference of opinion among them, some holding that Christ is a sinner and some the contrary. They appeal to the man who was blind, and he expresses the conviction that Jesus is a prophet. Later they return to him again saying: " We know that this man (Jesus) is a sinner." At this the man who was blind retracts his former opinion, saying, "Whether He be a sinner or no, I know not: one thing I know, that, whereas I was blind,

---

[1] St. Mark ix. 38.
[2] Cf. Micklem, op. cit., p. 134: "It is true that the patients seem to have been cured of their symptoms by a trust in the healer and a belief in his ability to heal them without any thought of God's activity in the matter."

now I see." When the Pharisees have left him Jesus returns and asks him: " Dost thou believe on the Son of God?" He answers: "Who is he, Lord, that I might believe on him?"

We notice that immediately after his cure the patient shows no particular interest in Christ's identity; his attention is entirely absorbed in the simple fact of his restored vision, and he informs his neighbours that he was healed by " a man called Jesus." It is not until the Pharisees' questions have aroused his interest and curiosity that he daringly surmises that our Lord is a prophet. Fearing to offend the Pharisees, he retracts for the moment even this modest estimate. He fails to see the fairly clear implication of Christ's question regarding his belief in the Son of God, and accepts our Lord's divinity only on a categorical assurance. Surely no one will be so bold as to say that this man was healed by a belief in Christ's divinity when he knew nothing of Christ's divinity until after his healing had taken place. And so it was with the ten lepers. Only one gave any indication that he recognised Christ as the Son of God, though all possessed the type of faith requisite for healing.

If we leave the Gospels and appeal to the experience of St. Paul we find a similar process in operation.

" And at Lystra there sat a certain man, impotent in his feet, a cripple from his mother's womb, who never had walked. The same heard Paul speaking; who, fastening his eyes upon him and seeing that he had faith to be made whole, said with a loud voice, Stand upright on thy feet. And he leaped up and walked." [1] The effective faith was " faith to be made

---

[1] Acts xiv. 8-10.

whole "—not the correct appreciation and acceptance of Christ's Deity.

But we can approach the same subject from another viewpoint. It is a significant fact that Christ's spiritual teaching was received almost with indifference in those very cities where His mightiest works of healing were performed. " He began to upbraid the cities wherein most of His mighty works were done, because they repented not. And thou, Capernaum, . . . thou shalt go down into Hades, for if the mighty works had been done in Sodom, which have been done in thee, it would have remained unto this day." [1] The communities in which His healing miracles were performed on the largest scale were precisely those which did *not* accept His teaching, which did *not* see in Jesus the embodied Son of God.

It seems, then, that the faith on which His healing depended was not of a theoretic or dogmatic character, but rather a confident expectation, amounting to certainty, that the thing desired and hoped for would actually take place. The idea of God's agency in the matter does not seem to have been a necessary condition, although Christ frequently informed those He healed that they owed their recovery to God. By faith our Lord did not mean an intellectual belief, but a dynamic power which provided its possessor with a direct supply of health and energy. And this faith expressed itself not in logical arguments and acceptances, but in action.

Christ's exhortations to faith were invariably made with the object of enabling people to *do things*. He reproached His disciples for the lack of it on those

[1] St. Matt. xi. 20-24.

occasions when they failed in action, when they failed to heal, to walk on the water, to feed the hungry.

Now this is precisely what M. Coué means by faith. Turning over the pages of his little book, *Self-Mastery,*[1] one is continually confronted by sentences such as this: "Be sure you will obtain what you want and you will obtain it, so long as it is within reason."[2] And again, "Conscious autosuggestion made with confidence, with faith, with perseverance, realises itself mathematically, within reason."[3] But, "when there is doubt, there is no result."

Let us appeal for a moment to our own experience. There are to-day millions of Christian people who possess an invincible belief in Christ's deity, who implicitly accept His teaching—as they understand it—and who passionately strive to realise it in their lives. How is it that this belief, this passionate willingness to do His bidding, remains without influence on their physical powers? The blind do not see, the lame do not walk, the dumb do not speak.[4]

But this is to be expected if the interpretation of "faith" which we offer above is a correct one. For while the churches to-day are full of dogmatic beliefs, they are not full of confident expectancy. And therefore the condition on which works of healing depend is absent.

[1] American Library Service.
[2] p. 38.
[3] p. 40.
[4] From this statement we wish to except the various methods of "spiritual healing" which have grown up in recent years, notably The Emmanuel Movement in America, and The Guild of Health in England. But it is our belief that the success of all these methods is due to an appeal—conscious or unconscious—to the type of faith we are discussing here, viz., confident expectancy.

CHAPTER IV

FAITH AND AUTOSUGGESTION

What thing is faith? . . .
Right well hath now been traversed this coin's alloy and weight;
But tell me if thou hast it in thy purse.
DANTE, *Paradiso* xxiv. (tr. Wicksteed).

WE have already seen (Chapter II), in the instance of the man with the withered hand, that a period of time elapsed between the initiation of the thought of healing and its physical realisation, and that this interval was utilised to increase and develop the patient's faith. A process psychologically the same though differing in the means employed is distinguishable in other cases.

We are told in Luke xvii that ten lepers appealed to Jesus to " have mercy on them, i.e., to heal them. Our Lord ordered them to go and show themselves to the priests, and, " as they went, they were cleansed." The Mosaic law demanded that when a leper recovered from his disease he must show himself to the priest to obtain, as it were, a certificate of restored health. Christ's command was therefore equivalent psychologically to this: " You are already being healed. Go to the priest that he may certify you to be clean." Thus at the same time He imposed a test upon their faith and supplied a means by which their faith could be raised to its full potency. For if the lepers refused

---

[1] We use the term *autosuggestion* throughout these pages in the wide sense in which it is used in the teachings of the New Nancy School. All suggestion which obtains acceptation by the Unconscious is here spoken of as *autosuggestion*. See *Practice of Autosuggestion*, p. 58.

to go, they had no faith, and therefore could not be healed. But if they obeyed Him the full realisation of what their journey implied would break upon their minds as they went, and this dynamic thought would heal them. This is precisely what happened, for " as they went, they were cleansed."

An exact parallel to this occurs in the case of the blind man to whom we alluded in the last chapter. Christ did not immediately cure him. " He spat on the ground and made clay of the spittle and anointed his eyes with the clay and said unto him, Go, wash in the pool of Siloam." [1] The spittle, the clay, and the washing were employed for their psychological effect. The man had not himself demanded healing; he had given no proof of faith; therefore Christ adopted unusual measures to arouse faith in him. But the faith thus generated was given time to develop. The thought of healing had to occupy and possess the man's mind. And so he was commanded to go to the pool of Siloam and wash there. Had he not had faith enough to go he would have been incurable as others were, " through unbelief." But his willingness to obey, to take his healing for granted, to act on the assumption that his vision was to be restored, in itself cured him, and " he came seeing." [2]

We see in these instances remarkable evidence of our Lord's psychological insight. We find Him adopting various indirect means to cultivate His patients' faith, to arouse that indomitable confidence which in itself had power to heal. Moreover we find Him exercising a subtle insight which recognised immediately the

[1] St. John ix. 6, 7.
[2] St. John ix. 7.

amount of stimulus needed to bring faith to the point of action.

It may be objected that in some cases Christ's healing was truly instantaneous. But if we examine them we find that this was always so when the patient, by speech or action, had given proof that his faith was already intense enough to heal, without undergoing further cultivation. We must remember that Christ's fame " went forth into all the land," multitudes of people came to Him to be healed and were healed; rumour and common talk spread the tale of His mighty works from village to village, from town to town. Impressionable people were thrilled with a sense of wonders on earth, touched by the thought of this great prophet or Messiah, " some said He was Elias, and some one of the prophets." Thus the woman who touched the hem of His garment[1] had heard stories of His mighty works, and had been fired by the thought that He could heal her also. She saw Him passing in the street, surrounded by a fervent and enthusiastic crowd; He was going, people told her, to raise from the dead the daughter of a ruler. With a passionate certitude of success[2] she followed Him, and forcing her way through the group touched His garment. It is scarcely accurate to say that Christ healed her: she healed herself through her faith in Him. Christ recognised this and expressed it clearly in the phrase: " Thy faith hath made thee whole." The cure resulted from a potent autosuggestion of healing which took place in the sufferer's own mind.

[1] St. Matt. ix. 20.
[2] Micklem, op. cit., p. 121: " We obtain a glimpse here into the faith which must have been hers to enable her to take the risk of the consequences of breaking a sacred convention and wilfully coming into contact with her fellow-men."

A few hours later, when Christ returned from the raising of Jairus's daughter, two blind men pursued Him through the streets, with entreaties for healing. They even obtained entrance to the house were Jesus was staying, insisting that He should heal them. Christ asked them whether they believed that He could do so, and when their answer showed their faith to be indeed sufficient, He " touched their eyes, saying, According to your faith be it done unto you. And their eyes were opened." [1] In these cases there was no need for the artificial cultivation of faith: the patients already possessed it. Their expectancy was already so intense that it could pass at once from a mental state into a physical act.

But if Christ healed by employing the natural human faculty of suggestion, what are we to say to the current belief that our Lord possessed a personal power of healing? There is no doubt that He did possess such a power. After the disciples had failed miserably to cure the epileptic boy, Jesus quickly restored him to health. Indeed, throughout the gospels we see evidences of the great superiority of the powers of healing possessed by our Lord. Yet Christ shows everywhere a preference for the normal human channels of action. He entered Jerusalem, not in a chariot of fire, but riding on an ass; He drove the hucksters from the temple precincts, not by summoning legions of angels, but by using the muscles of His own arms. And though He apparently wrought a miracle to feed the five thousand, He did not by a miracle obtain His daily bread. Indeed, He felt that such a suggestion was a temptation of Satan, and rejected it.

May we not seek for this healing power of Christ

[1] St. Matt. ix. 29-30.

among the normal endowments of humanity? We shall expect to find it developed in Christ to a far higher degree than is common among men. But there is no need to suppose that it was essentially super-human. As we have seen, the disciples shared this power in feebler measure with their Master, who regarded it, also, as a necessary endowment of those undertaking His ministry. He charged the evangelists He sent out to heal the sick as an integral part of their mission.

Christ Himself tells us that faith is as necessary to the healer as to the patient. On hearing of the disciples' failure to heal the epileptic boy, He exclaims: " O faithless and perverse generation! " [1] and He answers their inquiry as to the cause of their failure with the assurance that it was due to their " little faith." Only by prayer could they obtain supplies of faith adequate to the demand, and so when our Lord at the tomb of Lazarus was faced by one of the supreme tests of His own faith, He acknowledged the Father's answer to what was probably a request for an increased supply.[2]

Turning again to M. Coué, we find a parallel to this in the teaching of autosuggestion.

" Conviction," he says, " is as necessary to the suggester as to his subject. It is this conviction, this faith which enables him to obtain results when all other means have failed." [3]   And again, " Whoever the person may be who comes under your care; you can make

[1] St. Matt. xvii. 17.
[2] See Dr. A. E. Garvie: *Studies in the Inner Life of Jesus,* p. 230.
[3] Op. cit., p. 42.

something of him. Have the absolute conviction that you can make something of him." [1]

Is it not reasonable to suppose that Christ's personal power of healing consisted in His own immense and indomitable faith? Faith has a telepathic action upon other minds. One brave man will infuse a panic-stricken crowd with courage. And so Christ infected with His own faith the doubting minds of those who sought His aid. This being so, we find that our Lord did not preserve an inexplicable silence as to the nature of His own power. He spoke of it often and with all the definiteness due to so important a truth. He cease-lessly commended faith to His disciples as the means by which they, too, could perform mighty works. Now this power of diffusing a sense of confidence and faith is a natural power of the human personality. In greater or less degree it has been possessed by healers in all ages; and it is still the essential qualification of one who would enable others to heal themselves by awakening in them healthful autosuggestions.

But if the instrument of Christ's healing was that natural power of the human mind which we now call suggestion, if Jesus healed the sufferers who came to Him by kindling in their souls the unconquerable faith which was an attribute of His own Personality, how are we to understand His Nature miracles? The miraculous feeding of the multitude, the stilling of the tempest, the raising of the dead, the blasting of the fig-tree—all these seem inexplicable on any mental basis. They seem to demand the operation of a power superior to any power of which we are humanly cog-nisant. There will be some who will refuse to regard

[1] *Bulletin de la Société Lorraine de Psychologie appliquée,* 1er semestre, 1921, p. 19.

these miracles as authentic. But scepticism has received such rude shocks of late that the simple refuge offered by " I don't believe it " can no longer content us.

What did Christ Himself say? We are bound to admit that so far as He gives any indication of the foundation of these mighty works, it lies still in the same direction—faith. When the servant announced that the daughter of Jairus was dead, Jesus said: " Fear not, only believe." [1] When the storm threatened to engulf the ship on which the disciples were crossing the lake with their Master, " Jesus saith unto them, Why are ye fearful, have ye not yet faith? " [2] Even in reference to obtaining one's daily bread, one's shelter and clothing, Christ still commends faith. " If God doth so clothe the grass of the field . . . shall He not more clothe you; O ye of little faith? " [3]

Our Lord seems to have regarded lack of faith as a positive sin. Over and over again He rebukes His followers for the weakness of their faith; indeed it is almost the only failing for which He consistently blames them. Over and over again He teaches its necessity and enlarges on its power. " If ye have faith as a grain of mustard seed, ye shall say unto this mountain, remove hence to yonder place; and it shall remove; and nothing shall be impossible unto you." [4] As the healing miracles are now seen to be not magical portents, but the results of using the natural powers of the mind, so the time may come when these Nature miracles will be recognised as the utilisa-

[1] St. Mark vi. 36.
[2] St. Matt. viii. 26.
[3] St. Matt. vi. 30.
[4] St. Matt. xvii. 20.

tion of powers we all possess, but which are at present unrevealed to us.

Mr. E. R. Micklem advances one objection to our thesis in his valuable work, *Miracles and the New Psychology*. He assumes that suggestion cures are temporary in their effect, while the cures effected by Jesus were permanent, and therefore he concludes that Christ cannot have healed by means of suggestion. We cannot, however, admit that suggestion cures are merely temporary in their effect. It may be true that many of the cures produced by medical suggestion are impermanent, because no steps are taken to carry on the treatment in the form of autosuggestion, constantly renewed by the patient himself. Thus after the medical treatment is ended the old wrong idea begins to operate again and produces relapse. M. Coué, however, successfully guards against this by teaching the patient to repeat morning and night a general formula of health. And our Lord also provided those He cured with an effective safeguard against the recurrence of the complaint. He instilled into them " a new belief and confidence in the power and reality of the love of God "; that is, He implanted in their minds an idea which would operate in the future as a continual autosuggestion of goodness and health.

To sum up, we have seen that Jesus performed works of healing by arousing in the sufferer the autosuggestion that he was about to be healed. He did this by consciously utilising natural laws of the mind, which we are now beginning to investigate, and by conveying to the patient something of His own triumphant faith. We notice that in practising this method of mental healing our Lord shows a delicate psychological insight, an extraordinary power of gauging the potentiality of the sufferer's faith, and of devising the means best suited to raise it to the needful intensity.   In all this He utilises natural laws of the mind.   Indeed Christ was a psychotherapist, using in great measure the same means as the psychotherapist uses to-day, and using them with far greater effect.   But there is one fundamental difference.   Christ looked to God as the Source of His power; He appealed in His patients, not merely to a mechanism of the Unconscious mind, but to the health and power of God, who uses the Unconscious mind as a means of communication with our personal and individual lives.

CHAPTER V

PRAYER AND AUTOSUGGESTION

I say unto you, All things whatsoever ye pray and ask for,
believe that ye have received them, and ye shall have them.
ST. MARK xi. 24.

As we have seen, Christ regarded prayer as a means
by which we can obtain from the Father an immediate
gift of faith and power. Indeed, the faith was the
vehicle by which the power was provided. When the
disciples were confronted by a task of more than usual
difficulty they were to pray for faith, and with the
advent of faith would come the strength they needed.
This is, we believe, what Jesus did at the grave of
Lazarus. He prayed *for* faith and He prayed *with*
faith, and by this means acquired such mighty power
from God that He was able to free His friend even
from the bonds of death. The type of prayer Christ
commended was not the ostentatious and empty repetition habitual with His ecclesiastical opponents. It
was prayer made vital by the presence of faith; prayer
uttered with boldness and with the certainty of response. This our Lord lays down in one extremely
clear and definite pronouncement: " All things whatsoever ye pray and ask for, believe that ye have received them, and ye shall have them." [1]

The wording of this passage is remarkable. We are
directed to believe that we " *have* received " the objects
of our prayer and not that we shall ·receive them at

[1] St. Mark xi. 24.

some future date. These words have always been regarded as one of the most difficult and mysterious of
Christ's sayings, whereas they are one of the most en-
lightening. Commentators have given them scanty
notice, evidently regarding them as a mystical para-
dox or a confused interpolation. Yet nothing can be
more certain than that this is an authentic saying of
Jesus. Its seeming obscurity authenticates it, for
while copyists may soften down a hard saying, they
may safely be trusted not to invent one. But if we
are right in interpreting faith as a state of confident
expectancy this is exactly what we should expect our
Lord to say. It merely tells us that the mental attitude
of faith must be present just as much in our prayers
as in any other activity of life. Prayer is no isolated
exception. We must pray with faith, just as we live
with faith; we must preserve this dynamic mental attitude in praying as much as in doing. Thus, if we
pray for power, we have to believe that we are already
receiving the power; if we pray for purity, we have to
believe that we are already being made pure. God
answers us, even while we ask; " He knoweth your
needs before ye ask Him."

The belief that we are receiving already the benefits
for which we pray must always involve in some degree
the exercise of faith; yet sometimes it is little more
than the recognition of a psychological fact. The very
fact of praying for a spiritual quality is a sure proof
that in some measure we possess it already. Prayer
for a clean heart shows that in the depths of our being
the concept of, and desire for, a clean heart have
already formed; and what is a clean heart more than
a passionate desire for cleanness? This is what Pascal
meant when, in his *Mystère de Jésus,* he makes Christ

say to the human soul: " *Tu ne me chercherais pas, si tu ne m'avais trouvé.*" [1]   It is obvious that we could not pray for good unless we were good already—at least in some degree.   No evil man, *as such,* can sincerely pray for goodness: it is the goodness in him that prays.

This is not so, however, when the object of prayer is physical health.   Then God's answer depends entirely upon our faith.   We know that the presence of Christ, His words and His touch, sufficed to raise men's faith to such an intensity as to produce immediate healing. In prayer we come spiritually into the presence of Christ as surely as the sick of old time came into His presence bodily.   If, while we thus commune with Him, our faith is strong, if we believe that we are receiving the healing of our disorder, we shall indeed be healed.   This is surely the teaching of Christ, and cases of persons thus healed in prayer are not uncommon.   Physical healing and moral regeneration should be attained, at least partially, while the prayer is still upon our lips.

If faith is present in our prayer in sufficient measure the answer will be immediate, but in the nature of things we cannot always receive direct evidence of the answer.   We may be praying for strength to meet some coming event, to overcome some external obstacle which we are about to encounter.   Then, though our prayer should be answered while we pray, though we should at once receive the strength we need, we cannot be objectively aware of it until the time arrives to step out into the world and grapple with the difficulty.   So our faith will receive the additional task of

---

[1] *Pensées,* Edition Brunschwicg, p. 576.

sustaining us in quiet confidence until the moment comes for action.   During the interval we must live in the calm assumption that the power we have asked for is now at our disposal.   By prayer we acquire God's power, by faith we use it.   But one of the ways in which we use God's power is to acquire more of it, and therefore in prayer too the element of faith must be present.

This profound saying of Jesus reveals three weak points in our conventional notion of prayer.   The first is our complete failure to realise the importance of the presence of faith.   We do not appreciate the fact that faith is the channel of God's action; that He *cannot* respond to our prayer unless this means is offered. The second is the idea that a time interval must elapse between the prayer and its answer.   We conceive of God as the inhabitant of some remote Heaven, situate " beyond the farthest star."   Our prayers miraculously reach Him, but we do not presume to expect an immediate response.   We must allow a considerable period to elapse, and meanwhile all we can do is quietly to wait.   But Christ taught that the Divine Power is so near that as soon as we ask with faith our petition is granted.   " Before they call I will answer, and while they are yet speaking I will hear."

And thirdly Jesus teaches the inevitability of God's response.   " Believe that ye have received it and ye shall have it."   There is no question of God's refusal or of His referring our prayer back for further consideration.   Indeed, this absolute certainty of response is a theme to which Christ constantly returns.   " Ask and it shall be given; seek and ye shall find; knock and it shall be opened unto you."

The superficial resemblance between prayer and autosuggestion has often been noted, but when we consider the type of prayer which Christ commends to us in this passage, we perceive that the similarity is indeed profound. " Be sure that you will obtain what you want," says M. Coué, "and you will obtain it, so long as it is within reason." [1] The future tense used here does not truly express his meaning. We are told to say: " I *am getting* better and better," and in all specific suggestions " we should affirm that the change has already begun." [2] From this it is but a short step to the faith that we " have received " the things we ask for. The faith required in prayer and the confidence required in autosuggestion are so close to each other as to be almost identical.

Similarly M. Coué insists that autosuggestion, correctly performed, should immediately begin to produce its effect. This is most clearly apparent in his treatment of pain, which should disappear *during* and not after the treatment. It is true that in other forms of autosuggestion a time interval frequently elapses between the initiation of the suggestion and the appearance of the result. But M. Coué would attribute this delay to insufficient confidence or to the intrusion of effort. Correctly performed, autosuggestion should produce its effect at once.

And the parallel holds good in the inevitability of response. " Conscious autosuggestion," M. Coué tells us, "made with faith . . . realises itself mathematically, within reason "; for " whatever we think becomes true for us." Thus the three main characteristics of prayer, as our Lord understood and commended it—the need for faith, the expectancy of im-

[1] Op. cit., p. 38.
[2] *Practice of Autosuggestion*, chap. viii.

mediate response and the inevitability of response—
are also the three main characteristics of normal autosuggestion.

In reading St. John's gospel we find repeatedly that
Christ places one condition on the inevitability of God's
answer to prayer. He speaks of prayer in His Name.
We must believe that He means thereby something
more essential and profound than the mere addition of
the name of Jesus at the end of our prayers. Indeed,
it is generally recognised that by prayer in His Name
Jesus means that prayer must be consistent with His
character, it must be in harmony with the nature and
goodness of the God He revealed. He invites us to
test our aims, our ambitions, our desires, by the touch-
stone of His spirit, and to make them the subject of
prayer only when we find them in consonance, in harmony with it.

Now on a much lower level M. Coué's teaching provides a parallel to this. In the above quotation from
his book, *Self Mastery,* he restricts the efficacy of autosuggestion to such matters as are " within reason,"
and in administering suggestions to his patients he uses
these words: " You are going to have confidence in
yourself, and this confidence gives you the assurance
that you can do perfectly well whatever you wish to
do, *on condition that it is reasonable."* [1]   A thing is
reasonable only if it is in harmony with the laws of
life, and if it is in harmony with the laws of life, it
must also be in harmony, in a limited and human degree, with the laws of God.   But there is no need to
press this point unduly for we catch a glimpse of the
same principle in M. Coué's *Law of Subconscious
Teleology.* We are told there that in formulating par-

[1] Op. cit., p. 24.

ticular suggestions we must first see that their object is sanctioned by the reason, and, that being so, we must envisage the end and goal to which we wish to attain, making no attempt to impose on the Unconscious the means by which it is to be reached, but leaving all such questions of detail to be settled by the Unconscious itself. Autosuggestion should be as general, as undefined as possible. In its best form it should be an upward motion of the mind, fixing its attention on a goal universally approved, not spending its energy in personal likes and dislikes, in pursuing momentary egotistical desires. Is not the affinity obvious between this conception of autosuggestion and the rule which confines prayer to such matters as are concordant with the Divine Character? If God is goodness, a motion towards goodness is a motion towards Him.

Autosuggestion has sometimes been called praying to oneself. So it is; but it is prayer to a deeper, truer self, to what M. Coué calls "the power within." In our view that "power within" is God, whether we recognise the fact or not. God permits us to use His power, even when we deny that it is His power, just as a flower thrives in the sun without knowing the source of its vitality. And so when we formulate autosuggestions we are praying to God under the impression that we are appealing to some power of our own mind. It is sometimes said that according to the new psychology religion is nothing more than autosuggestion: we would reply that autosuggestion is nothing more than religion unaware of itself. Prayer, we submit, is an appeal, not to the God of some far-away Heaven, but to God in our own hearts; and, as such, it is indistinguishable from normal autosuggestion, except in one inestimably vital respect—the recognition of divine agency.

"Prayer, our daily prayer," says Dr. Horton,[1] "whether at set times or ejaculatory, should be in effect the constant autosuggestion of Christ's presence and Christ's sufficiency, and the assertion of faith that we can be like Him, and are by His grace, the indwelling of His spirit, becoming like Him."

[1] *The Mystical Quest of Christ,* p. 261.

CHAPTER VI

CHRIST AND THE WILL

> It is our will
> That thus enchains us to permitted ill.
> SHELLEY, *Julian and Maddalo.*

IN pursuit of our aim—the comparison of our Lord's teaching with the theory and practice of autosuggestion —we must inquire what was Christ's attitude towards the all-important question of the Will. We have been passing recently through a period of what might be termed idolatry of the Will. Moralists have combined to elevate it to a highly privileged position in the commonwealth of the mind; and in this respect at least their views have obtained ample support. Perhaps it is natural that the mental faculty which is identified with force should be highly esteemed at a time when force plays such a preponderant part in economic and national life. At any rate, the strong will has been popularly regarded as the most admirable quality of manhood and the shortest road to commercial success, and, since manhood and commercial success are marketable commodities, methods of cultivating the will have proved an excellent investment for the speculator. Let us, however, put popular prejudices out of mind and try to elucidate our Lord's teaching as revealed in the New Testament.

So far as we can discover Christ did not once recommend the development of the human will. He never advised its use as a means of attaining His Kingdom or deepening the life of the spirit. Indeed, so far as Jesus mentioned the will at all it was to insist in the strongest terms that the personal will must be given up to make way for the will of God. This is the principle He followed in His own life. He consecrated His entire being to doing the will of the Father. In His moment of supreme mental anguish He found solace and strength by surrendering His own will, and accepting that of God. " Not My will, but Thine, be done."

In truth we must confess that the modern conception of militant Christianity, with its " Onward, Christian Soldiers," its " Fight the Good Fight," its tendency towards rowdy and violent righteousness, is inconsistent with the teaching and example of Christ. It is true that Christ is sometimes reported as showing anger, but, as Miss Lily Dougall [1] points out, the emotion He experienced was probably a passion of grief. Nowhere among His sayings do we find a commendation of self-assertion; we search in vain for " blessed are the pushful "—we find only " blessed are the meek," " blessed are the peacemakers."

Indeed, the tendency to which many of us have succumbed to apply to the combative instinct for our religious dynamic has its root not in the teaching of Christ, but in that of St. Paul. [2] There is nothing in the life of Jesus which can be regarded as a justification of spiritual militarism, but there is much in the writings of St. Paul which seems *on a superficial view* to be in its favour.

Paul was a man of indomitable courage and unwearying energy; a man of action in the fullest and

[1] *Practice of Christianity*, p. 92.
[2] See A. C. Benson: *Where No Fear Was*, p. 216 f.

noblest sense. He constantly urged others to be as mighty a doer as himself, and he tried to show them how they might become so. But his writings contain nowhere any exhortation to attain spiritual progress by way of effort and strife; he makes no appeals to the will. On the contrary, the human will according to Paul is a failure.

His fascinating self-revelation in Romans vii. is a confession of the impotence of his own will, an anticipation of M. Coué's *Law of Reversed Effort*. It is the classic statement of the impotence of effort as a means of attaining a spiritual life. Indeed, Paul's watchword of justification by faith is formulated in flat contradiction of the idea that salvation may be gained by efforts of the will. We are to be strong, not in ourselves, but " in the Lord and the strength of His might." [1] This famous passage, which on the surface seems to glorify spiritual effort, will be found on closer examination to teach nothing of the kind. " The whole armour of God " contains only one aggressive weapon—the sword of the spirit, and that turns out to be " the word of God." The apostle conceives the Christian soldier, not " marching as to war," but standing confidently on the defensive, clad in the most peaceful of panoplies—truth, righteousness, the gospel of peace, faith, salvation (in the present) and prayer. We cannot agree with Mr. Pym [2] that " the noise of Paul's battle cries drowns Paul's teaching on faith." His military metaphors denote not effort but earnest desire. [3]

But in the teaching of Jesus there is no possibility

[1] Eph. vi. 10.
[2] Op. cit., p. 31.
[3] It is no part of the Christian belief that Paul was never guilty of inconsistency. We believe that the above is true to

of such misconception. He taught simply that we must give up our wills to God. Of Him it was said, " He shall not strive nor cry." He was the Lamb of God, distinguished for meekness, selflessness and humility.

But a misconception of the nature of this divine humility has given rise to a type of Christianity as faulty as that of the " Christian militarists." Christ has been looked on as weak and immature, interesting mainly to invalids and infants. Some Christians have attempted, in allegiance to this mistaken ideal, to annihilate their own personalities, to become flabby nonentities, the playthings of tougher natures, feeding secretly on sentimental yearnings. They delight in children's hymns of self-conscious sentimentality and picture Christ as a sensitive adolescent, with His lip a-quiver and tears ever ready to rise. Such are as wide of the mark as their brethren, the apostles of force. They have brought on the teaching of Christ the reproach of weakness and effeminacy.

For the negation of will which Christ teaches *is a means of acquiring greater power and energy than the personal will can ever provide.* We are to discard our weak personal wills, the discordant impulses of the ego, in order to set our lives in harmony with omnipotent being, so that we may attain to a strength far beyond our individual capacity. In our relation to the material universe we are constantly adapting our own wills to the laws of nature. We have been able to utilise immense natural powers, such as steam and electricity, because we have been willing to act in

the essence of his teaching on the will. As the Bishop of Manchester says in an article " Coué and St. Paul " (*The Pilgrim,* October 1922, p. 100), " The essential act of the will in Christian experience, as St. Paul described it, is surrender."

obedience to the laws by which these forces operate. In the mental and spiritual realms we encounter the same necessity.

If a man attempted to force an electric current to obey his will, to transgress the laws by which it is governed and submit to his personal desire, either he would obtain from it no force or it would destroy him. So if we would utilise healthily the power which God gives us through faith, we must obey the laws which govern that power, we must subdue our personal will to the divine and allow the divine power free action in our lives. If, on the contrary, we presume to utilise God for our own ends, to subdue His will to ours, and use His power in opposition to His will, either we shall be reduced by inward conflict to a state of impotence, or we shall become monsters of soul-destroying egotism. By yielding our will to God we live in harmony with the divine personality and our will, flowing in the current of the divine will, reaches for the first time its full stature.

The purely personal will can only rely upon itself. It therefore prevents the working of faith. A man has none but his own resources to fall back on, the small strength of his body, the little powers of his mind. Therefore, his faith cannot go far before it is brought up sharply by the reason. "Who am I?" he is bound to ask himself, "to attempt the working of wonders? I know I have common sense and a sound constitution, but this matter of removing mountains is fantastic. How can I presume to heal the sick, when Smith, a better man than I, makes no attempt at such achievements?" The exercise of the personal will, the ego-powers, reduces us to our own mean stature, strips us of the god-like nimbus, reduces us to futility. But the assumption of God's will by faith inspires us with the knowledge that nothing is impossible, gives us the means of drawing on the universal source, of transcending ourselves.

Therefore Christ exhorted the disciples to live in the power of God, and not in their own strength. " Be not anxious for the morrow "—rely, not on your own effort, but on God's power. " Ask and it shall be given," not struggle and the strongest shall take for himself.

All this would seem at first sight to have little to do with any theory of mental healing. But we find that the crux and storm-centre of M. Coué's theory is precisely his attitude towards the will. This is expressed in his well-known *Law of Reversed Effort*,[1] which runs as follows: " When the will and the imagination are antagonistic, it is always the imagination which wins, without any exception. In the conflict between the will and the imagination the force of the imagination is in direct ratio to the square of the will." [2]

The mathematical terms are, of course, merely metaphorical.

The wording of this law has frequently been criticised. We are willing to concede that for the English reader it is an advantage to substitute " thought " for " imagination." [3] It may be also that the use of the term " will " somewhat misleads the professional psychologist; it has been objected to by Dr. Wm. Brown and by the Bishop of Manchester. M. Coué uses the word in a popular sense, and means by it the exertion of conscious effort to overcome an obstacle—in this

[1] So named by Baudouin.
[2] *Self Mastery* (Allen & Unwin), p. 17.
[3] This is done in the revised edition of *The Practice of Autosuggestion*.

case an unwelcome thought.   In this sense it is used, with perfect clarity, by Dr. J. A. Hadfield,[1] and its convenience in the present discussion is, we think, self-evident.   This question of terminology is discussed more fully in *The Practice of Autosuggestion,* third revised edition, chapter v.

This teaching cuts squarely across the idolatry of the will.   Not that M. Coué denies the power and importance of the will, but that he subordinates it to a higher instance—thought; teaching that only when the will is obedient to thought can a man rise to the full pitch of his potential powers.   During the formulation of suggestions we must cease from effort, because effort is a utilisation of our conscious selves, while the very object of the suggestion is to appeal to greater powers behind and beneath the conscious self, to dip into fresh reservoirs of energy.   And during our daily lives we must avoid the appeal to the conscious will in order to appeal to something greater.   We must think, not " I, so and so, can do this in my personal capacity," but " the powers which dwell within me can do this, even if it is beyond my normal strength."   Surely it is obvious that in this matter the teaching of our Lord follows the same course as that of autosuggestion; that they are indeed identical, except in so far as Christ appeals expressly to the omnipotent God within the heart, while M. Coué appeals through thought to a power within, which he does not recognise as the power of the Father.

Christ approaches this same problem of the will indirectly from another angle.   He expresses His ideal in these terms: " Except ye turn and become as little children ye shall in no wise enter into the Kingdom of

[1] *The Spirit,* article "Psychology of Power," p. 87.

Heaven." Little children exhibit few of the qualities of the " strong-willed " man. A self-willed child is rightly regarded as a spoilt child. We expect the child, not to be feeble and lacking in individuality, but to be willing to draw its wisdom and strength from its parents, to act in harmony with the parents' greater knowledge. Surely this is one of the attributes of the child which Christ desires us to copy. We must rely on our heavenly Father in obedience and trust, as the child relies on his earthly father. We must not set up our own ignorance, our wrong perspectives, our partial sense of values against the omniscience and omnipotence of God.

As our Lord exalted the child so He consistently condemned the self-satisfied " intellectual." Whenever He met erudition He delighted in shocking it with the divine simplicities. To the learned Nicodemus He gave the staggering advice that he must be born again. His knowledge gave him no power to perceive or enter the Kingdom; he was to discard it as a hindrance and learn simplicity. He had to discover that his stores of information were beside the point. They offered no help in the spiritual quest, rather they distracted his attention, and caused him to miss the road. The opponents on whom Christ poured His indignation were the " intellectuals," the scribes and Pharisees, and their blindness justified His judgment. And still to-day the " meddling intellect," as Wordsworth calls it, is an obstacle to the attainment of the spiritual life. Instead of practising faith and charity we comfortably debate abstruse doctrines, and consider ourselves saved by our ratiocinations. We know too much, and often what we know is not worth knowing. We cannot see the wood for the trees.

Now Christ did not mean that erudition in itself is wrong, for He Himself was learned in the law, disputing even as a child with the doctors in the Temple. But He meant that the path of erudition does not lead to the gates of the Kingdom. Holiness comes of a simple affirmation in which pure reason has little part, and the more intellectual we become the more we rely upon the intellect and the less we are likely to act in simple faith. This would seem to be in harmony with M. Bergson's contention that the intellect is an instrument fashioned for utilitarian ends, and is impotent to aid us in the pursuit of spiritual truth. Certainly the experience of M. Coué and his practitioners harmonises with that of Jesus. The more intellectual a man becomes the more obstinately he seeks salvation in the use of his conscious reason, the less does he rely on the reasons of the heart. Intellectual people are as eager to grasp all the theories of autosuggestion as they are those of theology, but having obtained this intellectual comprehension they call a halt and in consequence their knowledge produces no real effect. Indeed, intellectual people frequently find that if they attempt to practise M. Coué's method their " meddling intellect " insistently intrudes; they try to perform intellectually processes which belong exclusively to the Unconscious mind.

An excessive development of the head to the detriment of the heart is as great an obstacle to the successful practice of autosuggestion as it is to the successful practice of Christianity. And so, too, Christ's puzzling preference for the child finds its parallel in M. Coué's experience. Emotion, intuition, imagination, play a more predominant part in the mental life of the child than reason and the critical faculties. The child is more trustful and possesses greater faith. M. Coué finds that the child is for this reason a more successful practitioner of autosuggestion than the adult—even as our Lord regarded him as in closer contact with the realities of the Kingdom of Heaven. The will is as great a problem to psychological science as it is to the churches. The psychology of the will is as little understood as our Lord's teaching on the will. Yet if we synthetise these three aspects of our Lord's teaching and inquire what place they occupy in the theory of autosuggestion, we find a body of agreement that justifies us in assuming a profound and far-reaching harmony between the psychology taught by Jesus and the psychology taught by M. Coué.

One important distinction must be noticed. Jesus, though His attitude to the will was a negative one, was continually teaching the need of an active desire. It is no good seeking a thing unless you want to find it. He asked the sufferers who came to Him if they wished to be healed before He proceeded to heal them. And desire is equally needful in autosuggestion. We cannot be cured unless we have a deep and active desire to be cured. We cannot achieve an improvement of mental or spiritual life unless we deeply wish for it. It is easy to confuse the exercise of the will, the making of effort, with this state of desire and aspiration, and no doubt such confusion has led to many misconceptions. But there is no real identity between them. We can desire a thing without attempting to obtain it by conflict and effort. We are most likely to secure the object of our desire when we have faith that we shall obtain it, and allow this faith to direct the course of our action.

CHAPTER VII

THE POWER WITHIN

Oh! never yet hath mortal drunk
A draught restorative,
That welled not up from the depths of his own soul!
GOETHE.

WHAT authority have we for assuming, as we have assumed hitherto, that God works within and through us, so far as we allow Him, to shape our lives to His purpose? It is self-evident that if God is omnipresent He must in some sense dwell in man; and since we are in closer touch with our own spirits than with objects of the material universe, it would seem that we come into the most direct and intimate contact with God when we seek Him within.

We must admit that on the question of God's immanence in man Jesus gave us but few explicit pronouncements. Christ was not a systematic theologian. The ultimate truths of religion, which have exercised the minds of theologians and metaphysicians since man first became capable of abstract speculation, are assumed by Christ without any attempt at intellectual proof. He nowhere sets out to prove the existence of God or the immortality of the soul; He takes them for granted; and in the same way He takes for granted God's immanence in the human heart. Christ's attitude to the Father was that of a son, not that of an analytical philosopher. He tells us of God's power and beauty and love, He does not resolve Him into constituents or enunciate Him in laws. What a contradiction it would have been had we found our Lord engaged in theological and metaphysical speculations with those whom He exhorted to be born again as little children!

Perhaps the greatest sanction of the doctrine of God's immanence in man lies in the fact that Christ regarded the Father as dwelling within Himself. In St. John's Gospel He declares that the Father within Him is the inspirer of His speech and the doer of His works (xiv. 10, 11). Whether we regard the discourses of the fourth Gospel as the *ipsissima verba* of Christ or rather in the nature of a paraphrase is of no importance here. We have at least Christ's meaning, and that is the vital matter, for " the letter killeth, but the spirit giveth life." By addressing ordinary men and women as His brothers and sisters Jesus implied that they were children of the same Father and that God's power and life dwelt in them too.

We are not left, however, without one completely satisfying and definite pronouncement on this question. When advising the disciples on their conduct when brought for trial before kings and magistrates Jesus speaks thus: " But when they shall deliver you up, be not anxious how or what ye shall speak. For it is not ye that speak, but the Spirit of your Father that speaketh in you." [1] No ingenuity can explain away the simple meaning of these words. They express beyond cavil the belief of Jesus in an indwelling God, and their record in each of the synoptic Gospels strongly witnesses to their authenticity.

If we can accept the authority of St. Paul there is no room for any further doubt. St. Paul teaches the immanence of God in man not only through the Holy

[1] St. Matt. x. 19-20; St. Mark xiii. 11; St. Luke xxi. 14-15; cf. 2 Tim. iv. 17.

Spirit, but also through the indwelling of Christ. We are here on mystical ground and we must beware of unduly rationalising things. If one may distinguish, it would seem that the apostle speaks of Christ within, when personal affection and loyalty to a living Master are uppermost in his mind; he speaks of the Holy Spirit, or the Spirit, when he is moved by the consideration of God's presence in its more general and universal aspect. Sometimes he combines the two, as in such a passage as: "If any man have not the spirit of Christ he is none of His." But, however this may be, there is no question of Paul's wholehearted acceptance of the doctrine of Divine immanence in man.

Faith in the God within gave Paul exactly those powers which Christ told us it could give. He was conscious of possessing within himself the resources of a Divine Presence. Consequently he displayed an immense and buoyant confidence. He was no pale philosopher, full of possibilities and peradventures. He was sure. He was certain. And he uttered his certitude in plain speech. "I know," he tells the Romans, "that when I come unto you I shall come in the fulness of the blessing of Christ" (Rom. xv. 29). Wherever he went the life of the people was stirred by his presence. The passing of a divine force manifested itself. His intensity of conviction, his strength to sustain fatigue of body and mind, the dynamic powers of suggestion which worked through his speech and presence, above all, his indomitable faith, give us a clear glimpse of the immense power derived from a belief in God's immanence in one's own soul. "Know ye not that ye are a temple of God and that the spirit of God dwelleth in you?"[1]

[1] 1 Cor. iii. 16.

But we must meet the objection that Paul seems to teach the Divine immanence as contingent on a state of conversion; that is, that God only dwells in us when we acknowledge ourselves to be His, and is absent from the heart of man in his natural state. This misunderstanding has found a place in Christian teaching ever since, but it bears the stamp of that separatism for which the Pharisee was condemned. Nevertheless it attempts to express an important truth, viz., that God only becomes free to act directly in our lives as we consciously and willingly submit ourselves to His influence.

The traditional conception seems to have been that when a man is converted, the Holy Spirit, coming from we know not whence, enters his heart and there dwells. Thus the converted person is essentially different from the unconverted, since he is a man indwelt by the Divine, while the latter is man pure and simple. We must, however, admit that there are various degrees of conversion, that we cannot set on the same level St. Francis of Assisi and the ordinary routine church-goer. And it would seem therefore that the Holy Spirit can dwell within us in infinitely varying degrees of completeness. But if this is so, when are we to say that He is entirely absent?

That science and religion are complementary revealers of truth is now an admitted fact; and we are justified in regarding the teaching of immanence from the scientific standpoint. Modern theology agrees that we cannot, in the name of common sense, conceive the converted man to be different *in composition* from the unconverted; we cannot postulate any essential element in the converted, which is not present—at least potentially—in the unconverted. Conversion is a new direction and outlook, rather than a new soul-substance. The conclusion is that God is present—at least potentially—in all men, that His power acts in us in natural law, but that when we recognise and accept His presence, we become true sons of God and His power can act through us with far greater directness and intensity.

At the same time the change from potential to actual sonship is often so far-reaching and profound that nothing short of obstetric metaphors can express it, and we speak naturally of a "new birth," of being " born again." In this way, no doubt, we should understand such statements of Jesus as that in John iii. 6. " That which is born of the flesh is flesh and that which is born of the spirit is spirit. Marvel not that I said unto you, Ye must be born anew." Prosaic theologians have pressed these words so as to make our Lord deny that man by nature, the " once-born " man—to use Wm. James's phrase—has anything of God in him. Certainly " converted " or " twice-born " men of a certain type have often taken pleasure in exaggerating their former depravity.[1] But a closer scrutiny of their confessions and a shrewder psychological judgment generally shows that in their so-called unregenerate life, God was still in some form present, that already they were seekers after the heights. Christ's words are not those of a lawyer drafting a will. They are metaphorical utterances in which absolute language is used for impressiveness, the necessary qualifications being assumed. Surely Christ is thinking of the qualities *predominant* in the two states—the fleshly and psychic before the " rebirth," the spiritual after. Only when we recognise it does God's presence

[1] E.g., John Bunyan.

burn within us like a flame, but " a spark disturbs our clod."

God's immanent presence is revealed most clearly not by processes of pure thought and speculative reasoning, but by personal experience. At all times men have been conscious of the divine in their souls in ideals, in inspirations, in conscience and in mystic visions. " It is . . . the presence of the infinite in our finite lives," says Dr. Pringle-Pattison,[1] " that alone explains the essential nature of man—the divine discontent which is the root of all progress, the strange sense of doubleness in our being, the incessant conflict of the lower and higher self, so graphically described by St. Paul as a law in his members, warring against the law of his mind."   But this state of doubleness is not the monopoly of the Christian; it is felt by all men in greater or less degree, for God dwells in all men, and not merely in those who subscribe to some special creed.   But the faith of the Christian is that when he recognises God's presence, and seeks to know His will and to do it, he can overcome this disharmony, and by a rebirth, a conscious replenishment from a higher source, become perfected.

Although the doctrine of immanence belongs naturally to the sphere of religion, yet science, and especially psychological science, is verging increasingly on the same conclusion. As Dr. J. A. Hadfield points out,[2] the great psychologists " have tended more and more to the view that the source of power is to be regarded as some impulse that works through us and is not of our own making. . . . Life and power is not so much contained in us, it courses through us."   We

[1] *The Spirit,* article "Immanence and Transcendence," p. 22.
[2] *The Spirit,* article "Psychology of Power," p. 110.

find that Janet speaks of "mental energy," Jung of "libido" or "urge," Bergson of "élan vital." No Christian can contemplate this universal power without relating it to God, without seeing in it one of the manifestations of God.

And so it is with the "power within" of which M. Coué constantly speaks. It is not part of our conscious selves; it is not bounded by the limits of our own personality, it is "a force of incalculable power which resides in each one of us." Inevitably one identifies this "force of incalculable power" with the "élan vital," the "urge," the "life-force," and through these with the transcendent power which is the gift of the Immanent God.

True, the view of science, in Coué and other psychologists, is a partial view. In the nature of the case it sees God as Power and not as Love. Yet perhaps this emphasis of God as the God of Power is not without its value for the churches. The New Testament record is suffused with a sense of power given to men, of a revelation of new sources of energy and strength. That sense of power has passed from the churches. It appears occasionally in the transient emotional intensity of revival meetings, but from the normal church life it is sadly though not entirely absent.

Nevertheless there are indications that the use of this power from within, even when its source is unrecognised, is accompanied by a tendency to other Christian virtues. It is as if we cannot "demonstrate" one attribute of God without being insensibly influenced to the demonstration of another. "Avoid anger," says Coué, "for anger only uses up our reserve of energy and enfeebles us . . . be calm, gentle, benevo-

lent." [1]   And again, " The altruist finds without seeking what the egoist seeks without finding. The more
good you do to others, the more you do to your-
selves." [2]   Is not this reminiscent of the words of
Christ: " Whosoever shall seek to save his life shall
lose it, but whosoever shall lose his life shall preserve
it "?

It is as if the use of God's gift of power from
within leads automatically to some perception of
Christ's moral teaching. Baudouin says: " To have
and to inspire unalterable confidence, one must walk
with the assurance of perfect sincerity, and in order
to possess this assurance and sincerity, one must wish
for *the good of others* more than one's own." [3]

We have tried in the preceding pages to discover the
bearing of our Lord's teaching on the contemporary
theory and practice of autosuggestion, and so to decide
whether the Christian is justified in practising the
method which M. Coué advocates. To this end we
have examined the teaching of Jesus in its psychological aspects. We have found every reason to believe that Jesus made use of the natural human power
of autosuggestion in His works of healing, and that
His teaching on faith, on prayer, on the function of
the will, and on the indwelling power of God was substantially in agreement with the theories on which
Induced Autosuggestion is based. If this is so one
can scarcely question that the Christian is fully justified in making use of this simple instrument of healing

---

[1] *Bulletin de la Société Lorraine de Psychologie appliquée,*
Ier semestre, 1921, p. 18.
[2] Ibid., p. 16.
[3] *Culture de la Force Morale,* p. 43. The English edition of
this work is *The Power Within Us.* (Dodd, Mead and Company.)

and self-culture. Indeed it may be cogently argued that the Christian is under a moral obligation to make use of it.

Autosuggestion in itself admits of no choice. It is a spontaneous activity which every human mind is daily performing. We can no more avoid making autosuggestions than we can avoid seeing or hearing. All we can do is control the direction of our autosuggestions.

It is recognised as a Christian duty to control the thoughts of the mind. Jesus identified thought with action and denounced the sins of thought with as much vigour as the sins of the flesh. And He did so because the thoughts of the mind, by the process of autosuggestion, *become* the sins of the flesh. Now Induced Autosuggestion is merely a method for directing our thoughts and thereby controlling their consequences. It offers us a potent means of securing the pure and ennobling thoughts which Jesus insistently demanded. Christ's censure on those who neglect to use God's gifts is clear and unmistakable. And having discovered within us a new talent, we risk His censure by ignoring it.

But we noticed that the suggestion made use of by Jesus appealed to something far deeper than a power of the Unconscious mind—it made a conscious and direct appeal to God's indwelling spirit. It is evident that the Christian who practises autosuggestion should follow the example of his Master, that He too should direct his appeal to God and so combine his autosuggestion with his prayer. This involves a reconsideration of the scientific method of M. Coué. It becomes necessary to consider its bearing on Christian practice and to find a place for it in the Christian life. In the chapters which follow we try to point out the means by which such an adaptation may be accomplished.

PART II
CHRISTIAN AUTOSUGGESTION

.

CHAPTER VIII

THE ALLIANCE OF CHRISTIANITY AND AUTOSUGGESTION

And is this little all that was to be?
Where is the gloriously decisive change,
The immeasurable metamorphosis
Of human clay to divine gold? . . .
. . . . is the thing we see, salvation?
BROWNING, *The Ring and the Book.*

THE human mind is possessed of a passion for unity. It cannot hold two ideas which are manifestly related to each other without striving to harmonise and unite them; and this harmonising impulse is the source of its triumphant progress. We may reasonably hope that the union of the elements common to both autosuggestion and the teaching of our Lord will yield a more perfect instrument than either has proved to be when used alone. This is not to say that autosuggestion adds to Christianity any potentiality which it does not possess already. There is no active power in autosuggestion which is not already present in the teaching of Jesus. But a knowledge of autosuggestion applied to Christ's teaching reveals in it a greater richness, a deeper meaning, than we have hitherto recognised. It enables us to see Christ's teaching on faith in its true perspective and to realise something of the immense practical value which it may have in our daily life.

We have already noted the superiority of Christ's healing resources over those of ordinary autosuggestion. The records suffice to show that Christ healed more rapidly and more completely: a word, a touch, from Him could open the eyes of the blind and loosen the tongue of the dumb. Religious healing, quite apart from that of Jesus, possesses resources which are not available to a non-religious mental method. The profound cravings for perfection, which implant in men's hearts a divine discontent; the emotions of love and loyalty; the courage and decision which enable a man to forsake all and follow Christ; all these add fire and potency to the faith which produces healing.

But what grounds can we adduce for faith in autosuggestion? We can be convinced of its truth by experiments, by the testimony of other persons, by the demonstration of a psychological process called the Realisation of Thought and of a dynamic called the Ideo-reflex Force. These things can be investigated and their truth is proved by evidence. But how weak is their appeal compared with the grounds of faith in God! Experiments awaken no emotion: the Ideo-reflex Force arouses no passion in our hearts. Our faith remains mere intellectual conviction and is lacking in dynamic power. And therefore our autosuggestions are apt to be feeble and tedious, and fail to bring the results we reasonably expected of them. The fault lies in our wavering faith, which never drew its nourishment from the deep supplies of instinctive emotion available in the Unconscious. It is evident that M. Coué's method alone, sound and valuable as it undoubtedly is, can never tap the full resources of faith which the human personality can offer.

But when we understand our Lord's teaching on faith we see autosuggestion no longer as an isolated scientific method; we perceive that in its essence it is a statement in psychological terms of a religious truth

—a truth which Jesus continually preached and illustrated by majestic examples. At once our attenuated faith in autosuggestion is reinforced and invigorated by our faith in God; it is able to draw on the deep springs of religious feeling; it possesses a sanction more satisfying than the most perfect scientific proof could provide; and thereby its efficacy is extended and increased. While still remaining in the category of psychotherapeutic methods it claims the added power of Christ's teaching and Christ's example. Therefore it is no longer limited to curing our bodily ills, to overcoming our despondencies and our tempers; it is recognised as the means by which Christ assured us that we could " remove mountains " and do " still greater works " than those He Himself performed. We do not wish, however, to hold out fantastic promises. Our souls are cramped and imprisoned by an environment which is full of doubt and negation. An individual can never realise the full potency of faith as long as he is surrounded with fear and with doubt. Even Christ could only preserve Himself from the infection of doubting minds by constant prayer and meditation, and there were times when He failed. In his own country, " He could do not many mighty works, because of their unbelief." The complete revelation of the power of faith can only come with the establishment of His kingdom. Nevertheless we can use it to-day in far greater measure than we have hitherto realised.

But not only does the Christian use of autosuggestion add new power to our practice; it also extends its scope. At present autosuggestion is mainly used for purposes of healing. It has proved effective in a high degree in the cultivation of moral qualities, but its application to matters of the spirit, without which morality is but shallowly rooted, is hindered by its lack of criteria and authority.   It cannot go to the roots of life, because its appeal is directed only to the halfway-house of the Unconscious mind.   When we realise its relation to the teaching of Christ we obtain at once the criteria and the authority we need.   Jesus offers us the moral and spiritual standards which the scientific method so sadly lacks.   Our autosuggestion must be governed by His teaching; its final goal must be the acquirement of His mind and spirit.   This being so we can apply autosuggestion in the most sacred and intimate affairs of life.   We can use it without doubt or scruple, because we are trying to do the will of God revealed by Christ and to do it by using God's gift of power.

But if the combination of religion with autosuggestion endows the latter with extended powers, we make bold to claim that it possesses a value almost equally great for Christianity.

In this new light we see that the true meaning of faith has been obscured and misinterpreted.   We have intellectualised too much.   True faith depends on a harmonious co-operation of conscious and Unconscious, but we have attempted to confine it to the conscious intellect and so have translated it into dogma, and replaced creative activity by creeds.   We do not even say: " I believe Christ "; we only say: " I believe *in* Christ," and we accept a vast number of ecclesiastical creeds and dogmas as though they were equal in value with the teaching of our Divine Master. Where in this repetition of dead men's beliefs, expressed in the language of a dead philosophy, is the dynamic energy, the triumphant doing, which Christ ceaselessly demanded?

We do not, of course, maintain that dogma and creed have no importance. Their importance is very great. A man's conception of the nature of God may decide his attitude towards life, the temper of his mind, the quality of his emotions. But the value of his creeds depends on the extent to which they are the expression of his own thought and the motive and dynamic of his life.

That this is felt by the churches we readily admit. The churches are conscious of their shortcomings and would willingly remedy them if they did but know how. But they have been carried along necessarily on the wave of intellectualism which has overwhelmed all other departments of life. As long as it was held that the human mind consisted only of what is called the " conscious mind " the churches naturally sought to win the soul by appealing to the highest faculty of the conscious mind, the reason to wit. But their appeal was without power, because it addressed itself to the head and not to the heart. A man convinced against his will is of the same opinion still, because only his head is convinced and not his heart, and " out of the heart are the issues of life."

Those elements in religious practice which an earlier age had adopted instinctively, such as the wise management of emotion through musical and pictorial art, fell into disrepute, at least in Protestant countries, because they made no appeal to the reason; while the intellectual superstructure of religion was over-emphasised and over-developed. And so, in place of the divine activities of Christ, many of the churches dissipate their energy in providing secular attractions, in organising dances and whist-drives. In the lives of ecclesiastics and popular preachers we see few manifestations of spiritual powers. Their faith is not a dynamic but a belief. They are good men, and some have a gift of organisation, a power of popular appeal, and a profound knowledge of the uses of advertisement, which would bring them to the top in commerce or the professions. But where are the prophets and the saints?—the men who by their spiritual and Christlike vitality bring inspiration and healing by their very presence, and defy the antagonism of the vested interests of ignorance and falsehood? It is power, life, vital urge the church everywhere lacks. There is an abundance of intellectual culture. Opinions crystallised into dogmas are maintained and defended with a fervour worthy of a better cause. The churches are divided over opinions, because opinions hold the supreme place and the power of faith an inferior one.

Christ told us that if we have faith, if we calmly take for granted the Father's readiness to give us power, we can do anything; that our abilities and our actions are limited only by our doubts of God's willingness to succour. "We have within us," says M. Coué, "an immense power, by means of which we can accomplish whatever we wish to accomplish—provided it is reasonable—and whatever it is our duty to do." This, in simple form, shorn of dogmatic elaborations, is the message of Christ; but Christ spoke of this power as that of our Father in Heaven.

Here, then, is what the churches lack—divine power —and here is the way in which we may gain it—by the exercise of simple faith, which is autosuggestion, a channel re-opened afresh, after long disuse and the accumulation of intellectual refuse, by modern psychology.

But there seems here to be a danger. In attempting to establish a concord between Faith and Autosuggestion we may separate the two great elements in the teaching of Jesus—Faith and Love. In exalting the power of faith we may unwittingly diminish the power of love. In this case we should do more harm than good. In the long run the power of God could not alone satisfy us. Used without the love of God, it would lead us astray. Indeed, if we glance at present-day conditions we must admit that power is everywhere exalted above love, and we cannot set things right by still further increasing this disproportion. But the way of escape has already been hinted at. It comes by discarding the ego and setting our own will in harmony with the will of God. This, we believe, is analogous, is indeed identical, with the setting aside of the personal will, during the formulation of suggestions, commended by M. Coué. God gives us His power on condition that we submit our will to His will. But if we do this we cannot conceive that God's personality acting through us will be other than loving, or will inspire any attitude towards our fellow-men other than one of love. Mere autosuggestion by the Coué method of a general formula already seems to tend in that direction. Much more can we expect autosuggestion, through a direct appeal to God, to produce the virtues of love and charity in those who make it.

But this is not all. Autosuggestion may be, and should be, directly applied to the attainment of love. There can be no doubt that a state of mind wherein love and charity predominate is the happiest, most efficient and most peaceful of all states. Christ did not tell us to love our enemies merely to please God. He told us to love all men because only by so doing could we hope to attain to His peace and His joy. Christian autosuggestion should adopt as one of its chief aims the attainment of this Christ-like quality.

In his new book,[1] Dr. Horton writes as follows: " He who will use this power of Autosuggestion aright and will apply it to the one end of becoming like Christ, may so study Christ's life, may so think out its application to his own life, may so keep the Image of Christ before his mental eye, that, gradually but surely, that Image works out in character and conduct. Without knowing it his person and countenance may suggest Christ, and almost automatically, without particular effort or conscious struggle at the time, he may come to act in each situation as Christ would act, to speak what is in reality Christ's word."

It may be well to sum up the benefits which the fusion of autosuggestion and Christianity can confer on each other. M. Coué illuminates the teaching of Christ on these chief points:

1. We must carry our faith over into prayer. We must not supplicate with doubting minds for benefits we do not expect to receive, but grasp God's hand with confidence, assume that He will help us and act on that assumption.

2. God should have all the ways opened to Him both in our mind and our body. His overflowing vitality should be enabled to vitalise every thought and every cell. It is not enough to call upon God to do His will in us. We must affirm with faith that He is doing it already. Paul tells us that God quickens our mortal

---

[1] *The Mystical Quest of Christ,* p. 265.

bodies through His indwelling spirit.[1] God yearns for us, even with the intensity of jealousy,[2] that He may reveal His power through every avenue of our being, and when we practise autosuggestion, through an appeal to Him, we simply open the gates that the King of Glory may come in.

3. We must live in an atmosphere of faith, for by faith alone can life develop all its hidden powers to the full. Even a grain of faith, real faith, will work wonders. We have not faith unless we use it.

4. We can by the use of autosuggestion more fully obey the two great commandments to love God and our neighbour.

The following are the main points on which Christianity enlarges and intensifies autosuggestion :—

1. It provides a basis of faith far beyond anything a purely psychological system can provide.

2. It opens up sources of emotion which would otherwise remain closed, for religion is capable of sublimating and directing the instinctive emotions as no other power can do.

3. Christianity provides a criterion of what is truly good, thus avoiding the ambiguities from which a purely mental system can hardly be free. For what we personally hold to be good, may not be actually good; but the Christian use of autosuggestion provides us with a standard.

4. By appealing to the ultimate source of power, instead of to a mediate entity—the Unconscious mind, far greater power becomes available, and greater results may be expected.

[1] Rom. viii. 12.
[2] Jas. iv. 5.

CHAPTER IX

GOD AND THE UNCONSCIOUS

The God of all grace would never be present on the earth at all if he were not present with the wicked.
GEORGE STEVEN, *Psychology of the Christian Soul.*

WE have already come to the conclusion that the suggestions employed by M. Coué make use, though unwittingly, of powers of God within us. But the psychological appeal is addressed to the Unconscious mind, and we cannot help inquiring what is the relation of the Unconscious to God.

The Unconscious, as we know, is the seat of memory, the power-house where energy is provided by instinctive emotion, and the supervisor of our physical and mental processes. It is, of course, much more besides, but these are its main characteristics. What have these things to do with the nature of God? At first glance very little. We know that the memory records of the Unconscious are faultlessly exact and finally complete, a veritable "book of life," which under some circumstances we may read.

As a source of energy, also, the Unconscious manifests one essential attribute of the Godhead, viz., power. "Power belongeth unto God," and He imparts it to human lives. Micah, in the eighth century B.C., declared that he was "full of power by the Spirit of the Lord," and St. Paul that he could do all things through the strength of Christ, "the power of God" (Phil. iv. 13; 1 Cor. i. 24). Psychology has amply shown

84

that this Unconscious energy is that of the instinctive emotions, and if both the religious and the psychological view are to subsist we must see in the instinctive emotions the natural vehicles of God's power. That they may be used for purely physical ends is abundantly clear; in fact, they are meant to be so used. But it is instructive to notice that this energy has a tendency to express itself in higher and derived forms, and that this tendency towards "sublimation" must be satisfied, if life under modern conditions is to be happy and harmonious.

The crude instinct of physical sex seeks to express itself in creative art, in ideal love for a person or a group, in tenderness of a mother for her child or of a nurse for the sick. The instinct of curiosity impels the man of science to years of selfless labour in the cause of truth, or the discoverer to hazardous quests to the frozen Pole. The combative instinct in sublimated form leads men into crusades for social justice, for purity, for religious truth. The instinct of fear itself is sublimated into reverence and awe before the majesty of Nature or of God. We see, then, that the Unconscious is the seat, not only of power, but of power pressing upward, of power seeking the ideal. In this, surely we can trace the finger of God. The records of physical endurance under the influence of love and tenderness approach the miraculous. And this power, as Dr. Hadfield points out, is not to be summoned by the will; it comes like power from on high. And it need be followed by no fatigue; fatigue coming only with doubt.

Finally the Unconscious supervises every physical activity. Just as all the hairs of our head are numbered, just as no sparrow falls to the ground without our Father, so no minutest change can occur in the body without the knowledge and responsibility of the Unconscious.

We see then that the three main qualities of the Unconscious, knowledge, power and control, are qualities generally attributed to God.

But we must admit with equal candour that the Unconscious possesses also the qualities generally attributed to the devil. If the instinctive energies are capable of sublimation they are equally capable of degradation and perversion. If we accept its gifts and powers as sent us by God we must admit that these gifts and powers lend themselves as readily to evil purposes as to good. Any premature idea we may have had that the Unconscious is identical with God is thus shattered.

There is a profound idea expressed by Plato, by Swedenborg and by Emerson to the effect that Nature is a perpetual repetition of the same theme on successive planes; that, like a spiral, it continually recrosses the same spot, but on a higher level. In the mind, Emerson tells us, " is all the process of alimentation repeated in the acquiring, comparing, digesting and assimilating of experience. Here again is the mystery of generation repeated. In the brain are male and female faculties; here is marriage, here is fruit." [1]

Now it is obvious that we cannot *know* the relationship subsisting between God and the Unconscious mind. The most we can do is to construct a picture, a symbol, which for the moment may serve us. In the above idea of the natural spiral of life we find perhaps the symbol we need.

Man is made, we are told, in God's image, but we

[1] *Representative Men.* " Swedenborg: the Mystic."

cannot take this to apply to the physical body in more
than a mystical sense. We may, however, think of
man as the image of God by means of the following
figure: the physical body is the lowest turn of the
spiral, above it is the mental plane, where the same
phenomena occur in a new medium; above this is the
spirit, and then after more turns of the spiral, at the
apex, is God. Thus all is in His image, spirit, mind
and body, each in its way reflecting God's nature.
Thus the qualities of the human personality are the
qualities of Godhead, manifested at a distance and be-
dimmed by their remoteness from the Source. This
is, no doubt, pure mysticism; but can one by any other
path, approach the mystery of God's relation to man?

How comes the evil into man's nature? This age-old
puzzle rises afresh to confront us. At the apex of the
spiral we are all one in God, but, as we descend, the
element of separateness becomes more and more dis-
tinct. In spirit we may be almost one with other
souls, in mind we come close, but in the body we are
entirely separate one from the other, without possibility of mingling. And as this element of separateness enters in, so arises, too, the element of choice,
of Free Will. We can choose to follow separateness
achieved in the ego or unity achieved in God. God
can only manifest Himself in us so far as we allow
Him to do so. If we could not choose freely we
should be no more than the puppets of God, and in our
goodness would be no virtue. Unless we were free to
choose God, our righteousness would be of no worth.
So Christ did not compel men to come to Him, He
asked them to come freely. The necessity which gov-
erns our lives is the result of past choices—choices
made by ourselves, by our parents, by humanity as a

whole.   And God is the captive of this necessity; He can express Himself only through the channels we offer Him; by our thoughts we make Him free or bind Him prisoner.

Our thoughts are like valves through which the life of God passes into our separateness; they are channels through which God's energy becomes human action, and that energy supplied by God, we may direct at our choice towards good or evil.   Thus God is limited by our conception of Him, and we can even turn His energy against Himself.   In this sense it is true that man creates God after his own image, and so far as our own lives are concerned God is what we think Him to be.   Thus in striving for a true conception of God and in setting aside our own will to do the will of God, we liberate not only ourselves, but God also.

The Unconscious then, while it partakes fully of our selfhood, is as it were a stage on the road towards God, a vestibule into which God may be admitted or from which He may be excluded; but to which, if we would live at all, we must admit Him partially, and in some at least of His forms of manifestation.   If we do not admit the love of God we must admit something of His power—or we should die.

Now by the method of M. Coué we seek to admit more and more of the power and health of God to our normal life, but we ignore His love.   " There is a power within us "—true, but there is also a Love within us.   By the method of Christian autosuggestion we call not only on God's power, but on God's love to transfuse and fill us; we appeal not only to the mediate stage, the Unconscious, but direct to the Source, and we may, therefore, expect a response not only of greater intensity, but tinged with the love, the beauty, the joy, of God's own nature.

To claim that the channel through which autosuggestion derives its energy is that through which God communicates with the human soul, and, further, that this energy is indeed God's energy, even when we fail to admit the fact, may at first glance awaken a certain repugnance in the Christian whose mind is accustomed to dwell on the unsearchable profundity, the illimitable sublimity of the Godhead. The mind is still unwilling to admit that God subjects Himself to His own laws. And this unwillingness results from the old conception of a far-away Jehovah, with whom we are not in direct contact. But the doctrine of immanence teaches us otherwise. It teaches that God who formed our bodies and our minds created a channel by which He could constantly be with us. Our life is not self-contained. We make it so only by shutting ourselves off.

And because our life does not originate or end in ourselves we are constantly doing things we wot not of. The poet in his speech utters divine truth beyond his comprehension and in us are forces at work shaping ends we cannot conceive—just as the first ape-like ancestors of the race moved unwittingly along the path towards Shakespeare. Our birth and life, which seem so purposeless move towards cosmic purposes. The labourer who enters the town in search of employment obeys an impulse which is building social entities of which the individual is but a single cell.

> The hand that rounded Peter's dome,
> And groined the aisles of Christian Rome,
> Wrought in a sad sincerity;
> Himself from God he could not free;
> He builded better than he knew;—
> The conscious stone to beauty grew.[1]

[1] Emerson: *The Problem.*

Realising this we can without difficulty make the admission that God uses the normal channels of the Unconscious to reach our individual life. Those channels which seem so personal belong not to us but to God, and are entrusted for the nonce to our keeping. Is it strange that God should use His own?

CHAPTER X

WHY PRAYER FAILS

Choose thee rather to be meeked under the wonderful height
and the worthiness of God, the which is perfect, than under
thine own wretchedness, the which is imperfect; that is to say,
look that thy special beholding be more to the worthiness of
God than to thy wretchedness.

The Cloud of Unknowing.

IT has always been difficult for those who believe in
the efficacy of prayer to account for the fact that the
vast aggregate of prayer offered privately and in our
churches remains, so far as we can humanly see, without answer. With monotonous regularity, week in,
week out, we pray for peace—and the world is involved
in the greatest conflict in history, every civilised country is torn with economic strife and civil war breaks
out in many parts of Europe.

But are these prayers uttered with faith? Generally,
we think, they are not. How many people believe
that there is between prayer and its answer a relation
of cause and effect? The whole natural world is built
on law. Every action brings its inevitable consequence. Yet between prayer and God's answer we see
no such relation. We feel that a prayer may hit the
mark or may miss it; God may answer or ignore it.
The truth is that if prayer brings no response there is
something wrong with the prayer. And the fault lies
generally in the absence of faith. While we say our
prayer we do not believe that it will be realised, or we
do not sincerely wish it to be realised, or the words

we utter are destroyed by indifferent or negative thoughts. Unfortunately the official forms of prayer too often defeat their own object. They are strangled at birth by the very thoughts that parent them. How can I be made pure if my eyes are never lifted from the contemplation of my sins? Unless I see purity with the eye of faith I cannot attain it. If I am sick and desire to gain health by autosuggestion I must concentrate my attention on health and not on sickness. The same rule applies to prayer. But unfortunately even in the venerable and beautiful prayers and litanies of the English Church we do not obey it. It is almost impossible to believe that God has already answered our prayer for goodness and health while we are calling ourselves miserable sinners and announcing that there is no health in us. Neither can we believe in God's ever-present succour and strength if our thought is occupied with our own miserable insignificance and God's awful, far-away sublimity. If our prayer is to be fruitful we must think of God as the loving Father who anticipates our needs before we ask Him and not as some austere and distant potentate. Many of our prayers are so expressed as to imply not love and beneficence on God's part, but an almost implacable harshness of temper. When we cry to God with melancholy insistence to "have mercy upon us, miserable sinners," we express by implication a disbelief in His paternal love. Jesus told us that God's love was infinitely more tender than that of a human father, yet no child would insult an affectionate parent by raising a daily petition for mercy.

"Consider for a moment," says the Rev. Harold Anson,[1] "what sort of home-life that would be in

[1] *The Sin of Wailing,* p. 7.

which the children were for ever cowering down before their father and saying: ' O most merciful Lord, be kind to me; I acknowledge that I am but a worm: I cannot hope that I am worthy to have my breakfast; indeed I deserve to starve; I can only hope for my breakfast because of your extreme mercy; but still I dare to hope; you have given me my breakfast before; you have given others their breakfasts; you have a great name for mercy; you will surely not fall below it; if you give it me I will spend all the rest of the day praising your undeserved goodness.' When the breakfast came the child would probably have lost all power of digesting it; the father would feel deeply dishonoured at the child's untrustfulness; no true home could be built up on such impossible conditions."

But suppose that this appeal was uttered not merely when the children had committed some offence, but as a regular daily practice. The father would reply that he had heard all this before, that he was not deaf, nor stupid, nor inattentive, and consequently there was no need for repetition, that when he knew the needs of his children he could be trusted to supply them. And as days and weeks and years passed, and the daily entreaty still occurred, we can imagine this earthly father deserting his unnatural offspring and leaving them to fend for themselves.

To continue this parallel (which is one used by Jesus), we may ask ourselves how a child should act towards a loving father. Obviously the child should take his father's love for granted, and should assume that it will continue in the future as it has been in the past. If he alludes to it at all, it will be to express gratitude and thankfulness; but the best repayment he can make will be to repay love with love, trust with trust, and to make the utmost use of the gifts and help he receives. And so we must act towards God. We must acknowledge His goodness, with faith take for granted its continuance, and see that we use the gifts of God to the utmost limit of our powers in doing His will and advancing His Kingdom.

It is a well-known fact of psychology that the surest way of developing any particular quality in one's character is to allow the mind to rest on it in contemplation. Thus the effect of continually regarding oneself as a sinner is that one becomes a sinner.

Suppose a man suffering from neurasthenia proceeded to formulate autosuggestions of this type: " I am a miserable neurasthenic. My life is a burden to me and to my friends. I am no good for anything. My mind is utterly morbid, and I have no power to resist the diseased ideas which constantly occur to me. Nevertheless, autosuggestion can help me if it will." Such a practice could only aggravate the evil, and he would probably end in a lunatic asylum. Yet by an analogous form of prayer we seek to eradicate sin. And we are surprised when we fail. But such a method is bound to fail, for its psychological basis is utterly unsound.

The lives of many hermits and anchorites have been spent in ceaseless strife with sensual and depraved thoughts. This was the natural result of a conception of repentance which encouraged them to dwell ceaselessly on thoughts of their own sinfulness. When they were not desiring evil, they were fearing and abhorring it. In any case their attention and their emotions were fixed on sin. But those who forgot themselves in the contemplation of God's perfection were engaged in no such struggle. Preoccupation with

one's own sinfulness is as harmful to oneself and as
objectionable to others as preoccupation with physical
disease.   It is an unhealthy form of egotism.   " True
humility," says Dr. J. A. Hadfield, "consists not in
thinking little of oneself, but in not thinking of oneself at all."   Christians who spend their time in piously
belittling themselves are certainly not making of themselves " vessels of the spirit."

And yet the state of mind we are considering, the
conviction of the worthlessness of the self-nature, is
incontestably a most valuable one.   Our egotistical individual self is without doubt a miserable sinner and
has no health in it.   Of ourselves we can do nothing.
Until he has recognised this the Christian cannot attain
to any measure of goodness, indeed he cannot be a
Christian at all.   He must experience this sense of
individual powerlessness, he must be willing to condemn the ego and desire to free himself from its
bondage, he must undergo remorse and repentance.
But the ego is not our whole self; there is in us also
the Divine Spirit, the source of all health, and the ego
is a mere abstraction unless it is thought of in combination with the indwelling power of God.   So when
we say there is no health in us, we must be careful to
limit this statement to our narrow self-nature; for to
say there is no health in our wider self is to say there
is no health in God.   When we have once recognised
the worthlessness of the individual and separate side
of our nature, we are free to pass on, to recognise our
potential perfection through the spirit of God within
our hearts.   Indeed, we must so pass on, or we shall
remain always in the destructive stage and never reach
the constructive.   Once we are convinced of our powerlessness to help ourselves, we must go on to the con-

templation of God's limitless power to help us. Otherwise we shall get no help.

If we return to our example of the neurasthenic we find the same principle. In his case, too, a preliminary knowledge of his own imperfections is necessary. Without it he could never become conscious of the need for healing, of the desirability of practising autosuggestion. Indeed, it may be expedient for his cure that he undergo a process of mental analysis, in which the full extension of his trouble is revealed to him. This is the psychotherapeutic stage which corresponds to repentance. But if he remains in this preliminary stage and never passes on from the recognition of his weakness to that of his salvation he will never be cured; on the contrary, he is likely to get worse. It is worth noticing, too, that when once the patient has recognised what is wrong with him he should not again return to the thought of his failings, but keep his attention directed to the qualities he needs and desires.

We now perceive repentance is not prayer but only a preliminary to prayer, and it should have been completed before the action of prayer begins. Nor should the stage of repentance be continually renewed and re-experienced for the same sins. Once we have recognised that our health lies solely in God, once this conviction is firm in us, we should pass on finally to the use of God's power and love by continually repeated acts of faith, by living in a faithful state of mind. We find that in the service of the English Church there is such a progression. We pass from confession to absolution. But the point we must emphasise is that when once the individual has recognised his own powerlessness and turned away from it, he should not turn back to it again, for by so doing he will hinder his own progress. Once he has become aware that he is a miserable sinner he should proceed to the full and continual recognition that he is the temple of the Holy Spirit.

We claim that this was the teaching of Jesus Christ. He did not recommend St. Matthew to pass his time in rueful contemplation of the sins he had committed as a publican: he was to follow Christ and spend his days in the quest of the Kingdom. The woman taken in adultery was to go *in peace,* and sin no more. If Christ had wished her to revel in the pains of remorse, to indulge in tears and anguished pangs, He would not have told her to go "in peace." Jesus called for repentance not from those who had already turned to Him, for they had already repented, but from those who had not yet recognised the need to follow His call. In the *Pilgrim's Progress* we do not find that Christian returned for a daily tub in the Slough of Despond. He got out of it as quickly as he could, and made all haste to reach the Celestial City.

On these grounds and others which were stated in a previous chapter it seems best, when once repentance has taken place, to turn resolutely away from the thought of our personal weakness, to dwell in the thought of our power through God. Prayer, as we have seen, is the means by which we acquire this power, and we can acquire it on condition that our prayers are uttered in the faith that we shall obtain, indeed that we have obtained, the strength and virtue we need.

We shall proceed in further chapters to consider how this general principle can be carried out in detail.

CHAPTER XI

SCOPE OF CHRISTIAN AUTOSUGGESTION

I still believed what Mr. Tell-True had said, and that carried
me beyond all.

BUNYAN, *The Pilgrim's Progress.*

WE have already seen that God can answer our prayers
only if they are uttered with faith. But it is difficult
to pray with faith if the form of words we are using
itself conveys a sense of doubt. There is an obvious
contradiction between phrases which merely entreat
God to help us and the belief that He is actually doing
so. Words are not only expressions of thought, they
are also pilots of thought. If our words are full of
doubt, how can our minds be full of certitude?

It would seem that the only means of ensuring the
presence of faith in our prayers is to use the language
of faith. And if this is so we must not be content
merely to *ask for* the benefits we need, we must also
use words, which, as it were, concrete our belief that
we *have received* them. The form of petition does
not suffice in itself; it must be supplemented by affirmation. Indeed, the affirmation would seem more
necessary than the petition. This method was used by
the writer of the Twenty-third Psalm. He does not
say, "O Lord, I entreat Thee to be my Shepherd;
I pray Thee to deliver me from want." He boldly affirms his faith with the words: "The Lord *is* my Shepherd. I *shall not* want. He *maketh* me to lie down in
green pastures. He *leadeth* me beside the still waters.

He *restoreth* my soul," and so on to the end.   The
psalmist is not looking back on a long life and recount-
ing what God has done for him; his mind is full of
the present and future, and what he desires of God
he affirms that God is giving him and will continue to
give him.   His prayer and its answer are bound firmly
together by faith.   It is hardly necessary to point out
that this is nothing more or less that the Christian use
of autosuggestion.

Our Lord's prayer at the sepulchre of Lazarus is
also an example of the form of prayer we are advo-
cating.   " Father, I thank thee that thou heardest me.
And I know that thou hearest me always."   Standing
by the open cave, before there is the least sign of the
restoration of the dead man to life, Jesus thanks the
Father for hearing His prayer.   We are not told
the nature of that answered prayer, but as Dr. Garvie
points out,[1] it was probably a request for confidence
and faith.

So far we have considered prayer only in relation to
our personal betterment, to securing and maintaining
health and the spiritual qualities which Christ commends to us.   But there is another type of prayer which
deals with matters external to ourselves, with the succour of some beloved friend, with the corporate life of
the Church, the nation or the world.   It is obvious that
in these cases the simple exercise of faith cannot immediately secure the answer.   Other lives are in question; there is more than our personal psychology to be
dealt with; in the Church or the nation an immense
number of different individuals are involved, and
therefore the response cannot be immediately supplied
by the channel which we call in science autosuggestion.

[1] *Studies in the Inner Life of Jesus,* p. 230.

Miss Lily Dougall [1] would therefore have us regard prayer of this nature as a separate activity, beyond the range of Christian autosuggestion, and related to it only in so far as both consist of a desire directly expressed to God. But we cannot lightly accept such a distinction.

Let us assume that I have to live or work with a person between whom and myself there exists no natural sympathy. We feel a constraint, even an active hostility, as soon as we come into each other's presence. My life may be rendered miserable and unfruitful by this unspoken feud. I turn to prayer as a means of escape. Has faith no part in this prayer? Is the devotional use of autosuggestion forbidden? According to Miss Dougall I shall intercede with God to remove the barrier which exists between us, but I shall not trouble to believe that He has done so, for I am using a type of prayer unrelated to autosuggestion, demanding power not from within but from on high. Meanwhile I still feel that the other man is an objectionable person; I still feel that " we can't get on together," that there is something which obstructs any advances which might bridge the gulf. Under these circumstances my prayer, I submit, will not lead to very much. But suppose, on the contrary, I recast my prayer in an autosuggestion form. Having asked God to remove the antipathy which exists between us and to replace it by His love and understanding, I give God thanks that He has heard my prayer. I affirm that as Christ loved all men, so I love my neighbour, that Christ's spirit is in him as it is in me, and that that spirit responds to itself. Therefore I like this man;

[1] *Guild of Health Quarterly,* Michaelmas 1922. " The Distinction between Prayer and Autosuggestion."

I am at ease with him, and he, in virtue of Christ's spirit within, likes me, and responds to all that is good in me.[1]

The next time we meet I shall approach him in a different state of mind. I shall carry with me a cordial atmosphere. Unless he is particularly callous he will respond and a new link will forge itself between us. We shall at least be able to tolerate each other; but as I continue my prayer daily, we shall pass far beyond this point; we shall become friends. Christ told us to love our enemies. This baffling command, seemingly so impossible, regarded throughout the centuries as an unattainable ideal, now comes nearer to us, and the means by which we reach it is the dual action of faith and prayer.

Let us go farther into this field which would seem to be reserved for intercessory prayer alone. Suppose that a man deeply interested in international justice, with a strong conviction of the futility of force, sets out to pray for the League of Nations. He intercedes with God on its behalf, but without the exercise of faith. Is he justified when his prayer is uttered in doubting the efficacy of the object of that prayer, in expressing the opinion that after all the League of Nations is a feeble institution and the hearts of the

---

[1] Dr. Horton in his *Mystical Quest of Christ,* writes thus (p. 262): "To attain Christ's love of all men, suggest to yourself that it is possible to look at men through His eyes, rather than your own; suggest that you do, as a matter of fact, renounce your own feelings in favour of His, your own judgment of men to make way for His." Then "you meet your old enemy and you find you love him, a great miraculous nimbus, a golden nimbus, seems to enwrap him; you see him in another light altogether; you are reconciled. . . . The autosuggestion has released powers within you, powers which assuredly come from the God of Peace, and these powers, not your own will, have produced the change."

peoples desperately wicked? Is not this to render his prayer an idle word, a mockery of the Father's power? The effect in the case of one individual may be small, but imagine the millions in all countries pursuing the same course—praying with doubting hearts, unbuilding with their thoughts what their lips have built. The League of Nations exists only by the active faith of individuals. If this faith died the League would vanish into thin air.

Everything, no matter how good, has its dangers, and intercessory prayer is no exception. We are tempted to think: " I have prayed. I have done my part. It is now in God's hands; so I have no further responsibility." He must, to save us trouble, intervene from heaven. Now the prayer of faith, which is Christian autosuggestion, precludes this. We are appealing to the Immanent God who works through us; and through us He will answer our prayer. When we have uttered our petition for the League of Nations, we thank God that His response is already given, and we affirm that God *is using us,* and will use us in greater measure, to spread its principles and champion its spirit. If we are unwilling that God should answer our prayer through us, if we do not wish to be made the champions of this cause, then it is doubtful whether we are justified in praying at all.[1]

It is true that one individual acting thus in utter faith might make himself ridiculous—but he would certainly make himself heroic. Think of an inspired clerk or insurance agent setting out single-handed to offer combat to the embattled forces of militarism. If he fought in the strength of the Lord he would not fight

[1] See on this subject an excellent chapter in Miss Maud Royden's *Prayer as a Force.*

wholly in vain. It is thus that the great movements of history were initiated. Thus were the slaves freed. The man whose faith was sufficient for such an enterprise could obtain from God by that very faith the qualities which would empower him for the struggle. A tentmaker and a fisherman carried Christ's word to the Gentiles and laid the foundation stones of the church.

But it is when we consider, not an individual, but a community banded together by one common aim that the full force of such prayer becomes apparent. Imagine the millions who pray on days of prayer for the League of Nations beginning to act in utter faith in its efficacy, regarding themselves as the living instruments through whom God will firmly establish it. Can we doubt that such corporate active faith could fail of its aim?

It would certainly seem that this dual form of petition and grateful affirmation should be used in all cases in which we are willing to be of service to ourselves. We can expect then that God will answer our prayers, in some measure at least, through us, and that we shall be made the channels of His response. If we are able to help and are unwilling to do so it is questionable whether we have the right to intercede at all, for how can we do so sincerely if we wantonly close one of the main channels of God's response, viz., ourselves.

Miss Maud Royden brings this out forcibly in her book *Prayer as a Force*.[1] As she truly says, prayer for others has the effect of revealing to us unsuspected ways in which we can help them. No prayer should be offered for others unless at the same time we offer ourselves to God as agents whom He may use for its

[1] p. 104.

answer. For God helps men very largely through men; and though we may see no way by which He can use us, yet there may be ways of which we know nothing. We sometimes sing of God's rich and boundless resources, but we forget that we ourselves are counted among these resources. Is not this what Paul means when, in Ephesians i. 18, he speaks of God's inheritance in the saints? One of the present writers once attended a service at which intercession was made for money—money needed for the work of a church. Man after man knelt down and asked God earnestly to provide the money. But they failed to realise that God *had* provided the money: it was jingling in their pockets as they prayed!

" More things are wrought by prayer than this world dreams of." We do not know, except in simple cases, the way in which prayer acts, and we do not know the limits of its power. Even when we seem entirely impotent to help, God may find some way of using us. If we possess the faith that our prayer will be answered, though the way of its answer may be mysterious and obscure, there seems no reason why that prayer should not be expressed in the language of faith, why it should not be cast in the dual form of petition and grateful affirmation. But the necessary condition of all prayer is sincerity; it must be unto us according to our faith. We should affirm that God is answering us, only if our faith is strong enough to meet the demand, only if we truly believe that He is doing so.

CHAPTER XII

THE CHRISTIAN FORMULA

Fill thy spirit with the ghostly bemeaning of it without any special beholding to any of His works—whether they be good, better, or best of all—ghostly or bodily . . . not looking after whether it be meekness or charity, patience or abstinence, hope, faith, or soberness, chastity or wilful poverty.
Cloud of Unknowing.

THE main practical difference between M. Coué's method and that put forward by other systems of a similar nature is that M. Coué advocates a general formula, while New Thought, Christian Science, and ordinary medical suggestion work by means of detailed and specific suggestions. This difference is of fundamental importance. M. Coué claims that his formula suffices in itself to bring about the healing, without any reinforcement on points of detail. "Do not seek," he says, " to make diverse suggestions, ' Day by day, in every way, I am getting better and better ' covers everything." [1]

The reason for this preference is not far to seek. The Unconscious mind in its function of supervisor over all our physical and mental processes possesses a knowledge of our true needs infinitely more reliable than that of the conscious. If I suffer from a headache my suspicion as to its cause is as likely to be wrong as right. Even medical science can make little more than an expert guess at the causes of some of our symptoms. But the Unconscious mind knows—

[1] *Bulletin de la Société Lorraine,* 1er semestre, 1921, p. 19.

knows without any shadow of doubt. It is therefore far better to leave the Unconscious mind to diagnose the trouble and prescribe the antidote. By means of a general formula I inform the Unconscious of the destination I desire to reach, leaving the way thither to its knowledge and discretion. I offer the Unconscious, as it were, a blank cheque, limiting it only, if such can be called limitation, in that the development must be *good* and *in every way*. Thus improvement may come at points where I should not have looked for it, or perhaps even desired it; for most of us possess pet weaknesses, favourite failings, which, if the process were under our conscious control, we should exempt, and retain for our private satisfaction. But a general formula forces us to choose all or none, to get better in every way, or not to get better at all. The ethical advantages of this form are even more self-evident than the medical.

When we look at this question from the standpoint of religion our preference for a general formula receives still further sanction. In consciously directing this general appeal to God's indwelling spirit we are, in the most literal and active way, subordinating our personal will to the will of God. So, in the religious practice of autosuggestion, a general formula will still retain its central and predominant position, but we shall consciously relate it to God as the Pilot of our lives. No other form can express the same complete trust in God, the same willingness to accept His will without condition or limitation.

Admitting then that we need *a* general formula we must now ask ourselves how far we can utilise the formula propounded by M. Coué. This formula, " *Tous les jours, à tous points de vue, je vais de mieux*

en mieux," is simply rendered into English as follows:
"Day by day, in every way, I'm getting better and
better."[1]   Obviously it consists of three main affirma-
tions: (1) *I am getting better,* (2) I am getting better
every day, (3) I am getting better *in every way.*   Is
there anything here which the Christian can regard as
inconsistent with the tenets of his faith?   Is it the desire to get better; or the wish to get better every day,
that is to say regularly and continuously?   Is it the
desire to improve in every way—mental and physical
and moral?

We take it that the time is now happily past when
the Church regarded the flesh as the essential enemy
of the spirit.   It is true that the flesh may be the enemy
of the spirit, just as the spirit may be the enemy of
the flesh.   But that there is any need for such a conflict we must emphatically deny.   If still there be
Christians who see in a healthy body a menace to holiness, we must ask them why Jesus devoted so much of
His short life to strengthening and restoring this subtle
enemy of His own ideals.   If disease and invalidism
are a precondition of Christian goodness, why did
Jesus wage such ceaseless war upon them?   Surely
He should have striven to strengthen the cleansing influence of disease instead of eradicating it.   Indeed, if
physical weakness and holiness are so closely related,
we must wonder why Christ Himself was not an in-
valid, why He made His entry into Jerusalem in the
prime of His vigorous manhood and not as a physical
wreck in a bathchair.   If disease and holiness are one,
then Christ should have been a pathological curiosity,
the triumphant incorporation of every disease and disorder with which mankind is blessed.

[1] *Practice of Autosuggestion,* chap. vii.

But He was not. We have no record of our Lord suffering from bodily weakness or disease. It is true we are told (St. Matt. viii. 17) that in Him an old prophetic oracle was fulfilled—"Himself took our infirmities and bare our diseases"; but no one supposes this to mean that He became actually afflicted in body. It was in sympathy that He took our infirmities, and He showed His sympathy in the most convincing manner by taking them away. Christ possessed perfect health, and if we would be truly Christ-like we must aspire to resemble Him in this respect also.[1]

> Let us not always say
> "Spite of this flesh to-day
> I strove, made head, gained ground upon the whole."
> As the bird wings and sings
> Let us cry, "All good things
> Are ours, nor soul helps flesh more, now, than flesh helps soul!"

It will be seen, then, that M. Coué's formula is well suited to be made the basis of our religious practice. The great objection the Christian must bring against it is that it fails to acknowledge that the source of its benefit is the Source of All Good.

It is obvious that if we recognise that normal autosuggestion in its essence consists of an appeal to God, we have already opened to it the religious resources of our nature, and in proportion to our belief in God's beneficence and power, will come an increase in our faith, and therefore in the efficacy of our practice. Thus if God's agency is once recognised and felt there is no need for a repeated reminder of it: one can proceed with renewed strength to the practice of M. Coué's method as it stands. In this case the recognition of God's agency will be mental, but not explicit.

[1] See Horton, op. cit., p. 258.

But it is doubtful if this will content us when we realise that Christian Autosuggestion is really prayer, prayer in which our faith is held fast in the form of words we use, prayer in which we literally obey our Lord's precept, and believe that we have already received the things we need.   Now, no one who practises the habit of prayer will be content to pray without explicitly calling on God for His succour and support.   And for such the formula of M. Coué must be verbally united to the concept of our Father in heaven. It is self-evident that there are innumerable ways of effecting this union, and that the Christian must be free to adopt the one which answers most nearly to the personal needs of his soul.   We shall do no more here than point out a few alternatives from which he can choose.

The simplest means of relating the formula to God is to introduce it by a short direct prayer.   Before our autosuggestion begins we can turn to God in terms such as these:

O God, our Father, I thank Thee for the knowledge of Thy love, Thy power, Thy readiness to succour, revealed in Thy Son, Jesus Christ; through Whom in simple faith in Thee, I can say: Day by day, in every way, I am growing better and better.

Or: *O God, our Father, grant that the words I am about to speak may be said in simple faith in Thee: Day by day, in every way, I am growing better and better.*

At the close of the prayer the formula would be repeated twenty times as in the secular practice.

This method will probably commend itself to those Christians who have already practised M. Coué's method with success, and would be loth to relinquish the use of his formula.

Another means of modifying the formula to our purpose is that of incorporating in it an acknowledgment of God's power.[1] A writer in the *Guild of Health Quarterly* [2] describes the experience which led her to the adoption of such a course and bears witness to its invaluable practical results. Her adaptation of the formula is well worth quoting and recommending. It runs as follows: *Day by day, in every way, I am getting better and better; through Thy grace, O Lord, I am getting better and better.*

Using this as a model, each of us can compose for him or herself a Christian version of the formula. In doing so we must guard against making it cumbersome and unhandy. Coué's formula is like a pebble, polished clean of redundancies, simple and round and smooth upon the tongue; thus its repetition has a lulling effect which reduces effort to a minimum and adds greatly to its effectiveness. Christian adaptations should be simple, short and rhythmical, should make no attempt at incorporating expressions of dogma, should be an appeal to child-like faith. Unless something definitely better can be found, the formula quoted above may be adopted as it stands, and will be found, we think, to meet the needs of the case.

But, as M. Coué points out, there is no special virtue in his formula, beyond its brevity, its simplicity, and its comprehensiveness. The formula of Christian autosuggestion may be something entirely unrelated to it, something more truly personal, which will express the aspirations of the individual soul. Several formulæ

[1] See *Practice of Autosuggestion*, chap. vii.
[2] Lady Day 1922.

have already been suggested. The Bishop of Manchester advocates the phrase: *Thy Will is my Welfare.*[1] This is simple and brief; it represents a high ideal of sanctity, a simple resolution to devote one's personality to the service of God. If one may venture to criticise it, it will be from the standpoint of general usefulness. Its value for health of mind and body does not seem so great as for personal sanctification, and we must seek for a formula which applies equally to all the needs of our life. If our conception of God's will is identical with that of Jesus, we have no fault to find with it. If God's will means for us health, goodness, joy, without doubt or limitation, this version is excellent. But unfortunately the ideas which cling to the phrase " Thy Will " in the mind of the average Christian are not all unexceptionable. We are so used to the fatuous exclamation, in face of some more than usually terrible calamity, " It is God's will! "—so used to this phrase as the last resource of the would-be comforter in time of trouble—that the idea of the " Will of God " is inextricably entangled with ideas of misfortune and disaster, things which are not the will of God at all, but the consequences of sin and folly. It would seem that those whose minds contain associations of this nature would benefit by a more explicit statement of God's beneficence.

Dr. Horton, in his recent book, advises us in considerable detail on this very point. He advocates that in the conception of Christlikeness we shall find a comprehensive aim which subsumes all our needs. " It may be reckoned that Christlikeness includes physical and mental health, for there is no sign that Jesus was ever ill, or ever suffered from any mental aberration.

[1] *The Pilgrim,* October 1922, article " Coué and St. Paul."

. . . To be Christlike means to be physically well and mentally sound, but also to be morally right and spiritually in unbroken communion with God." [1] He therefore commends to us the following general suggestions: " I am in Christ and Christ is in me." Alternatively one is advised to say on waking: " No longer I that live, Christ liveth in me "; and on falling asleep: " For me to live is Christ, to die is gain." Furthermore, we are at any moment of quiet during the day to utter the name of Christ and reiterate: " I can do all things through Him Who empowers me."

Thus, Dr. Horton tells us, the idea of Christ permeates the Unconscious and works through mind and will, as vital force works through bodily processes, " sets in motion power which resists temptation, stimulates to good actions, restrains from evil."

We see then that the choice of a religious formula admits of almost infinite variety. We are free to choose any formula from the simple phrase of Coué prefaced by a short prayer to an expression of the holiest and deepest yearning to share in the nature and spirit of Christ.

How are we to be guided in our choice? We must remember that the formula is a prayer, a prayer in the structure of which faith is organically expressed. And, since this is so, we can and must expect a response, for by rightly seeking we shall find. But the certainty of a response depends upon one condition— we must be absolutely sincere.

In the secular practice of autosuggestion we find that success is conditional upon what is termed " acceptation." Our suggestions are without effect if our Unconscious mind fails to accept them. Thus, if they

[1] Op. cit., p. 258.

are out of harmony with the emotional tone, if they run counter to any powerful Unconscious wish, there is a danger that they will be rejected by the Unconscious and so fail of their aim. This is equally true of our Christian autosuggestions. Throughout religious history this question of acceptance has always played a dominant part. Sacrifices were unavailing unless God accepted them; prayer was of no value unless God accepted it. But our prayers are not weighed at the judgment-seat of any distant and external heaven; God judges us in our own minds. Insincere prayers, prayers uttered with the tongue in the cheek, sentimental prayers arising from a passing fancy for saintliness, these never reach God at all; our own minds condemn them and refuse them passage. It is only prayers which express a deep and sincere desire that touch the Eternal Source and find their answer.

This fact is decisive in the choice of a religious formula. We must choose one into which will flow our whole soul's yearning. It is no good hiding from ourselves the fact that a desire for goodness is by no means universal. Some people are afraid that if they are good they will lose all the " fun " in life. They do not want to relinquish the favourite failings which they think make life worth living. And if, under the impression that ·they are performing a laudable religious rite, they recite a formula whose aim is complete Christlikeness, their Unconscious will pitilessly judge them, their suggestions, like their supplicatory prayers, will be mere movements of the tongue and agitations of the air.

Sincerity is of the first importance. We must guard against self-deception. Individuality is only rarely individual; most personalities are in some degree multiple personalities; at times one aspect is uppermost and we yearn for holiness, but at others we cannot breathe so rarefied an air and descend to lowlier levels. We must look to it then that our choice is not based on a transient mood, but is the most permanent and firm of which we are capable.

It is probably wiser to choose a formula below the highest level of our aspiration, so that even in duller and more commonplace moods we can still repeat it with sincerity. As our practice continues we shall grow in strength and be able to accept wholeheartedly a nobler formula of Christian suggestion. But at least for a beginning we should be cautious.

This Christian general formula, while it will not occupy so exclusive a position as that of M. Coué, should nevertheless hold first place in the practice of Christian suggestion. It should be repeated with unbroken regularity, without undue inquiry as to its effects, in a quiet persistency of faith.

Naturally it should be repeated at the times recommended by M. Coué; that is, just before falling asleep at night and immediately on awaking in the morning. It must be said without effort, in the state of child-like trust and faith which our Lord commended to us. The ideal state of mind would be that of resting like a tired child in the Everlasting Arms, losing oneself in our Father's love, and claiming that love for the supplying of all our wants.

CHAPTER XIII

CHRISTIAN SPECIFIC SUGGESTION

Still raise for good the supplicating voice,
But leave to Heaven the measure and the choice.
Safe in His power, whose eye discerns afar
The secret ambush of a specious prayer.
DR. JOHNSON, *Vanity of Human Wishes.*

ONCE having been convinced of the immense power placed at our disposal by autosuggestion, we may assume that nothing remains to be done but to go on formulating suggestions for all the various things we need, to fill our minds with a continual stream of induced autosuggestions. But such a practice would be very perilous. The same danger occurs in the case of prayer. All the masters of prayer oppose the practice of glibly praying for the satisfaction of every wish, and none more so than the supreme master of prayer —Jesus Christ. Much of His teaching was concerned with the question: For what shall we pray? The danger arises as soon as we pass from the *general* to the *particular.* In His model prayer Christ rigidly avoids details. We are to say, " Thy Kingdom come, Thy Will be done in earth as it is in heaven." But He leaves unsaid the specific means by which the Kingdom is to come and the exact manner in which the Will of God is to be performed. He implies that we must leave the details to God.

As we have already noted, M. Coué takes up a similar position in reference to autosuggestion. While admitting on the whole the value of occasional particular suggestions, he regards them with a certain disfavour, and why? *Because we are not wise enough to use them.* In physical matters there is perhaps less room for error; we know approximately what we want, and therefore we are unlikely to misdirect the Unconscious process to our own hurt. The danger lies rather in allowing our attention to dwell on the disease, instead of on the cure and so effecting an autosuggestion *à rebours.* But in dealing with mental qualities the possibility of error is much greater.

Our particular suggestions, if left to the choice of our own inclinations, may aim at the acquisition of qualities which are not truly desirable. We may mistakenly suggest what is pernicious, or what will destroy the harmony of our minds. Suppose a diffident man desires by the aid of autosuggestion to acquire self-confidence. His mental attitude towards a difficult task is a highly emotional and subjective one, his mind is obsessed by a multitude of doubts and fears. In this case there is a real danger that he will picture self-confidence as a similarly emotional and subjective state in which the negative feelings are replaced by those of blatant self-assertion. If his suggestions are realised he will find that he has forsaken the frying-pan to fall into the fire.

Indeed, the mental concepts we attach to words denoting generally applauded virtues are frequently faulty. How often do we call our personal uncharitableness by the name of candour, or our national uncharitableness by the name of patriotism? How often is lust described as love, miserliness as thrift, cruelty as just retribution? The rationalising faculties of the mind are continually at work whiting our sepulchres, ascribing flattering motives to our worst actions and calling our vices by virtuous names. It is clear that we must possess a safer standard than that supplied by the conscious reason if we are to avoid engulfing ourselves in self-deception, and setting the deeper forces of our nature in discord.

There is, however, another danger. In our search for harmony we may achieve it upon a low plane. We may attain to a harmony morally inferior to a noble discord, to the " sting which bids not sit, nor stand, but go." Suppose a discontented, moody person applies normal autosuggestion to the attainment of happiness. He will be tempted to make use of some such particular suggestion as this: " Every day I am growing happier. My mind is filled with pleasant, cheerful thoughts. Even if there is no definite, external cause for happiness yet I shall be happy; just as I have often in the past been miserable when there was no real reason to be miserable. Gradually this happy frame of mind will become spontaneous, and soon I shall experience it all the time." This is an excellent suggestion and will not be without its effect.

But it may be that this person is not leading the life he should be leading; that he is selfish, pleasure-loving, that his life is false and insincere, without value to himself or his fellow men. To be happy under these circumstances would be open to moral objection. Indeed, his unhappiness is itself due to a repressed impulse to be up and doing, to a timid refusal of the call of duty and conscience. Thus the success of his particular suggestions would be positively damaging to his character. Now the general formula would act otherwise. In obedience to the suggestion of growing " better and better " the impulses urging to action would probably be stimulated and happiness attained through worthy activity.

But it must be obvious that all disturbances which are due, at least partially, to causes lying deep in the soul will find their fullest solution only through the application of religion. We shall no longer be liable to mistake our true good, for in the life and teaching of Christ we possess a criterion, an example, which will make plain before us the path we should tread. It is especially in the case of particular suggestions that Christianity will solve our problems.

Many nominal Christians may not find this statement fully reassuring. They believe, though they may not admit it—even to themselves—that the teaching of Jesus is dangerously impracticable. They are afraid of being *too* good, lest, like the young man who appealed to Christ, they should be constrained to sell all they have and give to the poor. Their instincts rebel against such fantastic virtue, and they comfort themselves with reflections on the change which has taken place in economic conditions since Jesus roamed the hills of Galilee. This is not the place to consider a problem of such practical difficulty. We must confine ourselves to pointing out this fact: The most " fantastic " thing in the teaching of Jesus is His conception of faith. Yet after two thousand years of unbelief and miscomprehension we are compelled to admit that this teaching is in the best sense " scientific "; that it is an anticipation by twenty centuries of the newest discoveries in psychology; indeed, that it goes far beyond anything psychology alone can yet teach us.

How different might the history of the world have been if men had been able boldly to accept and practise that teaching when first it was uttered! If Christ's instructions had been executed in nothing but the healing of disease, how immensely higher would now be the standard of physique and of health in all traditional Christian countries. But if Christ appreciated so justly the true nature and power of faith, is it likely that He was wrong in other aspects of His teaching? May we not, even as practical, common-sense men and women, accept His doctrine in other directions?

But assuming that we are willing to make the teaching of our Lord the sincere and unquestioned goal of our Christian autosuggestions, there will still remain many questions upon which the New Testament sheds no clear and certain light. Problems will arise in our business relations, or in our political or social life, which confront us with two or more courses of action, to our judgment equally desirable and equally Christian, so that we do not know which to choose. In such a dilemma we shall appeal to the spirit of God within our hearts to give light. We shall dwell on the thought of God's infallible knowledge of the best course of action, and assure ourselves that He will reveal it to our minds. We shall ask God in faith to make known to us, during the course of the day, or on the morrow, which path we are to choose. And we shall then dismiss the matter from our minds, and wait for the solution. Indeed, no waiting is necessary; we can call on God for immediate illumination, and if we act with faith we shall obtain it.

We must now ask ourselves what form our Christian specific suggestions should take. We have to remember that in this category will fall our daily prayers —all prayer indeed with the exception of that included under our Christian formula and—possibly—of certain cases of intercessory prayer. Obviously one could logically proceed to recast all petitions in an affirmative form, and that is perhaps the boldest solution. Thus instead of saying, " Create in me a clean heart, O God, and renew a right spirit within me," we should say, *O God, Thou art creating within me a clean heart, and renewing within me a right spirit.* This is the most direct and indubitable expression of faith of which we are capable.

But many people will shrink from so sweeping a change. Prayer, the most sacred, the most intimate of human activities, is not a thing into which we can introduce sudden and revolutionary changes. The attitude of petition is so ancient, so hallowed, so rightly indicative of a humble and selfless frame of mind, that we cannot lightly part with it. And there is no need to part with it. It would seem that the most admirable method of prayerful autosuggestion is to ask God first in the petitionary form for the things we need, and then affirm with gratitude that He has already acceded to our requests, that our prayer has been or is now being answered.

Take the case of a man suffering from some physical disorder. He might proceed in such a manner as this: *O God, Thy will for me is health. In Thee is no fault and no blemish. In Christ was Thy perfection made manifest, an example for all men, and Thou wouldst have us perfect even as He was perfect. I pray Thee therefore to make me physically whole. Heal me now as Christ healed those who came to Him. By faith, O Father, I assume Thy healing; I grasp the good Thou holdest out for me. I thank Thee that Thou art healing me. I thank Thee that Thou art already granting my request and restoring me to health of body, so that I may be made more and more fully a channel for Thy expression.*

An analogous form would serve for any disease. There is no need to mention the specific failing; indeed, as we have seen, it is far better not to mention it, but to allow one's mind to go out entirely to the thought of the perfection manifested in Jesus Christ.

For worry, depression or any mental ill, we might pray in this manner:

O Thou, Who art unutterable peace, give me Thy tranquillity, Thy calm. Give me Thy peace, O Lord; the peace that was in the mind of Christ, the perfect calm through which His power was manifested. My Father, I know that what I ask in faith Thou wilt surely give me. And I thank Thee and praise Thee that Thou art giving me peace, that my mind is beginning to act calmly, surely; that Thy purposes in my life will be manifested with quiet power and certitude.

Or for purity: *O Thou, Who art purity and love; Who pervadest my being with Thy power and grace, I pray Thee to make me pure, to give me a love for all that is noble, sweet and true. Make me pure, in thought and word and action; that Thy spirit may act through me unhindered and unimpeded, and I may do Thy will. . . . I thank Thee, O Father, that Thou art purifying my heart, that Thou art even now making me purer, so that my life will every day bear the impress of a mind more and more filled with Thy perfection.*

One further observation is necessary. The supplicatory form implies the non-possession of the object of supplication. We do not ask for a thing we already possess. Suppose that yesterday we prayed for peace of mind, completing our prayer with the affirmation that God was now giving us peace; to begin our prayer to-day with the same petition is to admit by implication that our faith of yesterday was vain; or at least that its effect was transitory. We may thus be led to think that the supplies of strength and virtue we receive from God are valid only for twenty-four hours, and so our moral and spiritual life will lack stability. We may be assured, however, that God's gifts are in essence permanent, that they fail us only when we reject or misuse them. Therefore, when we have once obtained from God an increase in faith or peace of mind, that faith or that peace is ours, available not only for the momentary need but for future needs also. So on all future occasions we shall ask God not simply for faith or peace, but for *more* faith and *more* peace. Our prayers will be in the comparative degree.

We must remember, too, that God expects us to use His gifts, to use them immediately and in full degree. It is not enough, when we have asked God for some benefit and thanked Him for having heard us, to proceed in the merely theoretic belief that we possess it. We truly possess a thing only when we use it. We must grasp God's gifts with the hand of faith and proceed to shape our lives on the active conviction that we have them.

Let us assume that a man is restrained from public work by a sense of timidity and diffidence. His former efforts, say, to address a meeting have been accompanied by an agony of "stage-fright," which has rendered his work ineffective. He prays, therefore, to God for confidence, for the calm of mind which will enable him to control his thought, and to lose the sense of his self in the pursuit of his mission. And his prayer concludes with an expression of gratitude to

God that He has been answered and the needful confidence supplied. There is no doubt that that man will rise from prayer with a sense of calm power, a feeling that he possesses the confidence he has sought. But he must proceed on the first opportunity to use that confidence. He must believe that it will be his in greater measure, and in virtue of that belief, he must engage himself for the very activities which he formerly shunned. Thus his confidence, instead of remaining merely theoretical, will be put to the test of action and, sustaining that test, will be henceforth a normal condition of his life. So, too, if we pray for physical strength we must proceed to use that strength; we must use it even before we know that we possess it, for it is only by using it that we can prove to ourselves that we possess it. This is entirely in accordance with the canons of our Lord's practice discussed in a former chapter. The sufferers whom He healed were called on to act on the assumption that healing had already taken place. Thus the man sick of the palsy was told to rise, to take up his bed and to walk— to act as if he were healed; and when he acted so, he discovered that he was healed. The lepers were told to show themselves to the priest, and as they set off to do so they were cleansed.

So when we ask God for any gift we must proceed to act on the confident assumption that we have already received it; and if we do so with faith we shall find that we indeed possess it.

CHAPTER XIV

TEMPTATION

Through no disturbance of my soul,
  Or strong compunction in me wrought,
I supplicate for thy control;
  But in the quietness of thought.

WORDSWORTH.

LIFE is for most people a conflict; a conflict, not so much against external circumstances, as against rebellious powers in their own souls. We see " a different law in our members, warring against the law of the mind." " The horses of the soul's chariot," Plato said, " pull different ways." This inward schism forms the great drama, the great tragedy of life, and the achievement of peace has always been the soul's supreme quest.

This conflict appears in its most violent form in what we call temptation. It seems that outside us are two attractions, drawing us in different ways. But perhaps a truer view is gained by looking within. There we see two motives of our life grasping at the satisfaction of mutually opposed desires. For man is not one self, but many. He is a parliament rather than an individual, and a parliament in which the decisions are often approved on a minority vote and in the absence of many of the members. Temptation is a fight between two or more elements in our personality, each attempting to achieve control of our life, each representing a different ideal. The popular means of deciding this conflict is by making use of the Will. We resolve to fight the thing out to a finish, to defeat the evil desire once for all. We therefore call up all our forces; we do battle against the unruly desire; we dictate to it a humiliating peace, and we re-attain an equilibrium more or less unstable. But the defeated element continues unconverted. Its cause was to some extent legitimate, it was an attempt to satisfy an instinctive emotion, which, if no longer admirable, was so at some period of our racial history. This instinctive wish remains unsatisfied, and at the first opportunity resumes the offensive. Thus the schism continues, and our peace is perpetually menaced by new convulsions.

But suppose—though when the temptation is vigorous this rarely happens—suppose we defeat once for all this desire within us. Suppose the rest of us triumphs at its expense and holds it in perpetual thraldom. Then our total personality is so much the weaker and the poorer. We have lost in vital energy, we have lost in completeness of experience, we have made ourselves meaner and smaller than we need have been. We have, indeed, committed a partial suicide, analogous on the mental plane to chopping off a limb on the physical.

We have assumed hitherto that the higher powers of our life succeed in triumphing, at least for the time, over the lower. Such is by no means always the case. It may be that the primitive, the sensual elements in our nature outnumber, on this specific point, the moral components. In such a case the cause of righteousness would be defeated and we should yield to our temptation.

We have already seen that the issue of such a conflict is decided, in the main, by the thoughts which dominate our conscious mind. The conscious mind is the fortress, the point of strategic importance, which, once held, cannot be captured by assault. As long as the mind is obsessed with inferior or evil ideas the utmost efforts of the will still fail to dislodge them. Indeed, as is shown in M. Coué's *Law of Reversed Effort,* the energy brought up to attack and dislodge these ideas only serves to strengthen them. Our Will obeys our Thought; if our thought is evil, the powers of the will are directed to realising this evil. We can redirect the will towards good only by filling the mind with thoughts of good.

The drunkard whose mind is obsessed with a craving for drink and with images associated with the pleasures of drinking, finds that all the efforts of his will to withstand the temptation only hasten his steps to the nearest bar; but if his mind is filled with other thoughts the craving has no power over him.

The will has proved itself entirely ineffective to overcome temptation, except when it is directed by pure and holy thoughts. We know well that temptation itself comes always through thought and not through will. We are beguiled into sin by seductive fancies and suggestions. And it is by the same route that we must be led back to virtue.

It is obvious that the method of autosuggestion possesses the qualities best suited for overcoming temptation. It works not by conflict but by quietly replacing the evil thoughts by good ones. Continually and regularly presented to the mind, without effort or strain, the good thought tends to become habitual, the forces of the personality flow through this channel more and more strongly, until the course of action dictated by a sane and beautiful thought becomes one of the chief expressions of our life.

But thought only possesses dynamic power when it represents a desire. It has frequently been found that it is no good talking of holiness or of a Christ-like life to a person who is thoroughly depraved. He does not want to be holy; he does not want to be like Christ; and if thoughts of holiness remain in his mind they are merely a subject of ridicule. In such a case a lower ideal might prove attractive—the ideal of " sportsman-ship," or that of gaining the respect of his fellow men. This would be at least a step in the upward direction, from which further progress could be made later. There are multitudes of men who have no spontaneous desire for a saintly life, but who would like to be decent. And if we would strengthen and accelerate the effect of autosuggestion as a weapon against temp-tation we must systematically cultivate any desires we possess which are in opposition to that temptation. This will entail a little preliminary self-analysis to dis-cover the real nature of our desires.

Introspection—the analysis of one's own mental states—is frequently regarded as a sign of weakness. There is a type of mind which tends to brood in a subjective and emotional way upon its own faults. Such a habit is highly pernicious and damaging. The state of outcropping the Unconscious thus engendered causes the negative ideas to be realised as potent auto-suggestions and we increase the very evils we would be rid of. But there is another type of self-analysis in which we calmly and objectively take stock of our own natures, noting impartially our weaknesses and our powers, seeking to understand our true character and mental equipment. Such a practice has always been recognised as highly valuable. It helps us to clarify our thought, define our aims and achieve a greater measure of self-mastery. Above all we recognise what things we truly and deeply desire. This, of course, is the type of analysis required for our present purpose. But we must guard against the real danger that our objective analysis will degenerate after a few minutes into mere brooding.

A very simple stratagem will, we think, defeat such a tendency. We need but to take a piece of paper and write down the results of our self-examination. An example will help us here, and we will return to the case of the drunkard.

The drunkard then, at a moment when he is seriously inclined to make a bid for freedom, should take a piece of paper and write down in parallel columns a credit and debit account of his craving. This should be done in a thoroughly systematic way. He will allow himself, say, fifteen minutes in which to enumerate the advantages of the drinking habit and fifteen more to make a list of its evils. He must not suppress any idea which arises in his mind so long as it is relevant, and he must for the moment forbear from all criticism. The list is for his own perusal alone, and he must write with unashamed sincerity. In the credit column he will write, say: temporary forgetfulness of care, temporary exaltation and happiness, a feeling of enhanced power and greater manhood, a sense of comradeship with his fellow topers, the heightening of the capacity for sensual pleasures, etc., etc. To debit he will enter: injury to health, lack of efficiency in trade or profession, loss of self-respect and the respect of other people, anxiety and shame inflicted on those he loves, prospects of future misery, etc., etc.

When these lists have been completed he will read them quietly through. They will probably contain a good deal of repetition and he will proceed to edit them, so that each is comprehensively expressed in three or four items. On this basis he will construct a particular suggestion in which, while the credit items are subsumed under one phrase, the debit are mentioned individually. Thus: " Day by day, I am becoming more and more indifferent to the morbid excitement afforded by drink, and the habit is becoming repugnant to me. On the other hand, I desire increasingly to possess good health, to be able to respect myself and to win the respect of my fellow men. I love my wife and children more truly and unselfishly every day, and I deeply desire to do all that is for their good," etc. This particular suggestion will be repeated after the general formula night and morning, or at some convenient occasion during the day. By this means a man's desire for a saner, healthier life is fed and strengthened. As he attains a better mode of life his aspirations will mount higher, and if they do not spontaneously turn towards the Divine at least a favourable soil will be provided in which the Word, when it falls, may take root.

But the advantages of this little incursion into the sphere of self-analysis are not yet exhausted. The list of credit items—the pleasures and advantages of drink —will call for further consideration. If he has been truly sincere he will have gained a greater insight into his own character. He will be amazed that certain of the pleasures enumerated could have appealed to him as desirable. Unacknowledged desires, which the relaxed censorship has enabled to rise from the Unconscious, will be revealed to his conscious mind, and the immediate repudiation of them will go far to weaken their hold on him. Incidentally, this glimpse of his own weakness may well reveal the need of a higher power than he personally possesses and so lead him towards God.

But the desires which drove him to drink are all derived from instinctive sources, and are therefore not essentially evil. They reveal the fact that certain profound needs of his being are not being satisfied, and these needs may be capable of a higher and healthier satisfaction than that afforded by drink. In other words they may be sublimated. The temporary forgetfulness of care is one of the needs of life and can be met by other means than alcohol; the desire for fuller manhood is in itself admirable, so is the longing for comradeship. The man will therefore seek to discover new and unobjectionable channels for these instinctive desires. He can find relaxation from care in sport, in the drama, in music and art, in religion, in his home or in a useful hobby. Fuller manhood will come to him as he develops self-control and takes an active part in political, social or religious work; and these same channels will satisfy his desire for comradeship. Now with new aims set before him the energy which formerly impelled him to ruin will carry him upward into a freer, more harmonious life.

This same method, modified to the needs of the case, will prove of use in the overcoming of other forms of temptation, and any intelligent man or woman can apply it for him or herself.

Now it is obvious that the Christian in seeking to overcome a temptation is in a far stronger position than the secularist. For while the latter knows of no source of power outside his own mind and character, the Christian can appeal at once to the indwelling God, in Whom is an overflowing supply of faith, courage and confidence. He can appeal to God by the means outlined in a previous chapter—pray for strength and acknowledge its reception in grateful faith. It must be assumed that if he is a Christian at all he has a natural desire for goodness, and that, apart from temporary aberrations, this desire outweighs any appetite for inferior pleasures. If in spite of this he is liable to gusts of desire which overwhelm his better nature, it will help him considerably if he undertakes an orderly analysis of the nature of his failing on the lines indicated above. The debit side of his vice will be still more overwhelming than in the former case, since it will include the denial of all the ideals of Christ. Once more this analysis will be made the basis of prayer in an autosuggestion form and once more he will look for the means to sublimate the troublesome craving.

Let us suppose the sufferer is troubled by crude sexual desires. He must realise that this energy is capable of expression in higher forms than those of mere physical sex. Not that he will attempt the herculean task of sublimating his entire sexual instinct; he will sublimate only what is excessive in it. The sublimation will take the form of tenderness and care of those who are dear to him. If he is unmarried he will realise that when he finds a suitable mate he should marry. If he is already married he should without difficulty confine. his needs to the opportunities afforded by a tender and loving wedlock. This sublimation is a normal and healthy process. No power is more potent to achieve it than religion. The life commended by Christ is so full of opportunities for love that we cannot have enough love in us to meet them all. And this noble love and charity of the gospels is obtained by the raising and elevation of the instincts of sex.

The practice of Christianity does not involve the extermination of any element in our nature. There is in us no instinct which is inherently bad and must be eradicated. Every power we possess can be enjoyed to the fullest in the Christian life, but it must be raised from crude and elementary forms of expression to such as are consonant with the teaching and example of our Master.

Meanwhile Christian autosuggestion can remove at once any evil thought which may enter our minds. We must not, however, attempt to suppress it; on the contrary we must lift the mind—evil as it is—towards God. We must say to Him: " *Lord, it is not Thy will that I should think this thought. Take it from me, I pray Thee, and fill my mind with what is holy and pure. Fill my mind with pure, clean thoughts, O Father. I thank Thee that Thou hast heard my prayer and delivered me. I know that Thou wilt always deliver me when I come to Thee with faith, and, therefore, with the knowledge of Thy immediate succour, I have no fear.*"

We overcome temptation by cultivating the desire for its opposite. The rousing and sustaining of holy desires is one of the main functions of the church, and this duty is best performed by imparting ideas of the joy and power obtained in communion with God. Such thoughts create and strengthen desire. They produce the " hunger and thirst after righteousness " which are a blessing to their possessors, and which surely shall be satisfied. It is a good thing that the church to-day dwells so much more readily on the joy and love of God than it did in the past.

But Christianity offers us innumerable means of increasing the desire for goodness. The constant reading of the divine story of the gospels, the contemplation of the character of Christ, the thoughtful application of His teaching to our personal lives. All these are means of Christian autosuggestion by which the Christ-idea is realised in us with increasing strength, and the Holy Sp rit penetrates more deeply into every department of our being.

CHAPTER XV

THE CHILD

Sweet smiles, in the night
Hover over my delight!
Sweet smiles, mother's smi e,
All the livelong night beguile.
WILLIAM BLAKE.

ONE of the characteristics of our day is the increasing recognition of the pre-eminent importance of the child. We spend—and spend rightly—more and more money on its mental and physical health, its secular training and education. But there is, if anything, a decline in its religious training. The conception of secular education gains ground and the teaching of religion in the schools is often left to the discretion of a teacher who is an agnostic or an atheist. Parents who are themselves in the prevailing condition of mingled indifference and doubt on religious matters prefer to shelve a subject on which they find it difficult to be sincere. So that there is a tendency for the influence of religion on the growing mind to diminish.

It may be cogently argued that no teaching at all is better than bad teaching, especially on a subject of such supreme delicacy. And indeed we must admit that the religious teaching of the past was psychologically very imperfect. On the one hand there was the method, always a dangerous one, of bringing down truth to the level of the child's mind. No doubt a wise and gentle woman has often done incalculable

134

good by a tender presentation of our Lord's personality. But there has been also a vast amount of sentimentality. Too often, as we have already seen, Christ has been represented as a wistful puerile figure, a " gentle Jesus, meek and mild," hardly to be reconciled with the virile personality of the gospels. As the children grew they saw in this devitalised Christ a person far less admirable than their own vigorous, cheerful fathers. The boys, strongly desirous of being " grown-up," striving towards an ideal of manliness, soon outgrew the liking for such a figure and early came to designate religion as soft and unmanly. The reaction thus produced often exerted an influence lasting throughout life, producing an Unconscious identification of Christianity with weakness and sentiment, and of wrongdoing with manliness. One may well ask how much of the contempt for religion which exists among adolescents is due to the sentimental Christianity administered to them in childhood.

But the complementary method of imposing on the child abstract dogmatic formulæ is equally open to objection. The unfolding mind has a thousand problems of its own all pressing for solution. It is not yet sufficiently developed to comprehend abstractions. To expect it to grasp the doctrine of the Trinity or the nature of Redemption (when theologians themselves are struggling for light on such mysteries) is simply an abuse of mind. Children are incapable of understanding what we mean by such terms, and their efforts to do so produce anthropomorphic conceptions which would amaze their conscientious and ill-advised teachers. We have known a child who thought of the Holy Trinity as a three-headed man, and associated the Triune God with the photograph of some misconceived monster seen outside a travelling show. Obviously it is the child's thoughts that matter—not the words it learns by rote, however hallowed those words may be.

Current religious conceptions have often hindered and obstructed a child's natural growth in other ways. Many a child's early years have been darkened by a dread of God, derived from an acquaintance with the inexorable punishments chronicled in the Old Testament. He has lived in the fear that his own little sins and failings might be similarly visited. The prospect of the sun being darkened, the moon being turned into blood, has kept many little children awake at night. The all-seeing eye has been a nightmare to more than the boy who became Mr. Polly. Truly these specific fears are soon discarded, but with them are often discarded the invaluable truths; and not infrequently the habit of fear thus formed survives in projection upon other objects. Happily the old morbid insistence on Hell has given place before the growing conception of a God of Love. But these evils, so destructive to young minds, are still with us though in a diminishing degree.

Nothing is more regrettable in contemporary teaching than the cut-and-dried finality of our statements. We destroy the child's natural gift of wonder; giving it the impression that our little formulæ contain all there is of truth. And later, when he discovers their feebleness, he thinks the truth is not worth having, and throws away the pearl with the shell. Our attempts to bring God into the child's life by appeals to the intellect only result in distortion. Either we distort the truth before we give it, or the child distorts it on its reception. And yet Christ told us that to apprehend rightly His teaching we must become as little children!

Now when we speak of bringing God into the life of the child we mean infinitely more than giving a few intellectual concepts by which the little one may possess a provisional idea of God's nature. It is true that a child, with its restless curiosity, will demand such an idea. The means of satisfying that demand we cannot consider in the scope of this book. We would merely suggest that it is right to tell of God's love, His power and His beauty, and of His Spirit guiding and strengthening in our hearts; to make, as it were, a frame into which new detail will be added year by year, but so far as possible to abstain from giving anything which must afterwards be retracted. We should strive, not to satisfy the desire for the knowledge of God, but to feed it in preparation for days of maturity when the mind will be able to draw conclusions for itself.

Meanwhile the child needs more than ideas *about* God. It needs God's power and might and beauty in its own life. By what means can we satisfy that need?

Before considering the means at our disposal we must first point out that in a very true sense the child already possesses God's gifts. It is born with an unobstructed mind; with hereditary tendencies, no doubt, to sin and weakness, but without that mass of negative spontaneous suggestions, individual impressions of sin, disease and unhappiness, which clog and cumber the adult mind. There are no barriers to break down, no impediments to clear away. Wordsworth was right. The child comes "trailing clouds of glory," or perhaps transpired with the life which has come direct from God. Our first duty is to guard that innocency;

to allow, so far as lies in our power, no cloud of wrong-thinking to veil its depths. But in the nature of things we cannot do this in a merely negative way. We cannot bleach our thoughts and feelings and present them to the child grey and neutral tinted. We can only prevent our influence from being negative by making it truly positive. We must surround the young life with influences of health, joy, hope, happiness; then there will be no room for misery and disease to enter.

Now it is generally admitted that the temperament and character of a child is influenced, to a considerable degree, before its birth by the thoughts and feelings of the mother.[1] In other words, the suggestions, spontaneous and induced, which are made by the mother act not only upon herself, but upon her unborn child. The practice of Christian autosuggestion is therefore available not only for her own benefit, under the particular circumstances, but also for that of the new life she bears. This knowledge carries with it an immense power and a responsibility equally great. A' saintly mother might thus help to fashion a prophet and seer of the future. But it is questionable how far one is justified in so determining an independent life. Prophecy is a hard calling, and entails to-day as in the time of Elijah, both danger and persecution. The extent to which this privilege should be utilised must be decided by parents for themselves. The only general advice one feels justified in giving is this: The expectant mother should avoid ideas of sin, disease, weakness and misery, and should, in her thought, conversation and reading, dwell on all that is pure, beautiful, and strong, on those concepts which represent the unblemished gifts of God to man.

[1] See Baudouin, *Suggestion and Autosuggestion,* pp. 92-95.

In addition to repeating her Christian formula night and morning, she should make at these times the following Christian suggestions: the new life in her keeping is God's gift, inbreathed by God's life and love; it is God's will that this young life should be perfect, and as she yields freely her own will to God, God will accomplish His purpose through her. Therefore the little one will be strong in body, healthy in mind; its character and personality will unfold harmoniously and vigorously, and as the child becomes mature it will achieve, in obedience to God's will, a deep and peaceful spiritual life.

If during the day some harmful impression is conveyed to her, she should pray to God for the health of mind, body and soul of herself and her child, claiming. God's answer by faith, and offering thanks for His help. But the mother should not exaggerate the sense either of her power or responsibility; she should live a normal, healthy, cheerful life, knowing that she and her child are amply safeguarded by her morning and nightly practice and by her occasional prayers during the day.

The sense of the sacredness of motherhood is deprived in Protestant countries of one of its highest sources of inspiration. The churches insist strongly upon the Virgin Birth of Christ, but to Mary they have not given, so it seems to us, the place of honour that is her due. In avoiding the Roman Catholic conception of the Queen of Heaven, Protestant churches have gone to the other extreme and regarded her merely as the passive and neutral vehicle of the Holy Child. But unless the natural laws governing birth and childhood were completely set aside in the case of our Lord, Mary must have been a woman of unequalled wisdom, serenity and beauty of character. Can we for a moment conceive of Christ as the son of a coarse, insincere or frivolous woman? She was adorned, said Luther, with a wreath of three fair roses: faith, humility, purity. And these qualities were reflected in her Son.

After the birth of the child the mental influence of the mother is obviously not so direct and exclusive as it was before. But of all the influences around it the child will be normally most susceptible to that of its mother. The mother should therefore take care that she harbours no wrong thoughts, no malice or evil temper, no anxiety or gloomy forebodings. On the contrary her mind should be stayed on the thought of God's mercy and love and care. If at this time any of the little ills to which infancy is subject should arise the mother should take the little one on her knee and, gently caressing the affected part, quietly pray to God for help in some such terms as these:

"*My Father, I pray Thee to give my child health, to strengthen it in body and mind, to remove this present ill and restore my child to health and strength. Thou hast told us, Father, that whatever we ask in faith Thou wilt grant us. Father, I have faith in Thy power and Thy willingness to heal. I know that Thou art healing my child even now, that Thy ineffable power is already at work bringing him back to health. Thy will for him is health and strength and beauty, and Thou art doing Thy will at this moment in the mind and body of my little one.*"

The mother may continue thus in prayer for some minutes, dwelling without effort on the thought of the perfect health which is God's will, thinking of her child as having already been healed. Meanwhile, if medical aid is necessary she should certainly avail herself of it.

There can be no opposition between medical care and treatment and healing by prayer. The physical means of healing are as much God's gifts as the mental or spiritual, and we should make use of them all for the attainment of our purpose.

After birth the child registers directly the emotional states of all who come in contact with it. The character of the nurse is therefore of the utmost importance. It is not sufficient for her to possess a knowledge of the needs of children and an adroitness in satisfying them. She must have a cheerful healthy mind, or her influence will be pernicious. Psychoanalysis shows how often children have been injured for life, mentally and morally, by ignorant or depraved nurses.

Perhaps the most effective means of applying Christian autosuggestion for the benefit of the child is as follows: When the child is asleep the mother should enter the room, taking care not to awaken it, and in a whisper formulate some such suggestions as these: *" God's will for you is health and strength. His will and His power are manifested in you more fully day by day. Therefore you are becoming strong and vigorous in body, your mind is developing in a perfectly healthy manner, and you are becoming a good, sweet-tempered, happy child. Every aspect of your life is growing and unfolding rightly, the spirit of God is manifesting itself in you more and more, so that when you grow up you will be a true disciple of Christ, courageous, unselfish, strong and gentle."* If the mother prefers it these suggestions could be uttered in the form of a prayer, a petition to God which ends in an affirmation and a giving of thanks. Should the child be ill her suggestions will be directed to its restoration to health. One might repeat a dozen times the phrase *" God is healing you! "* and then pass on to enumerate the benefits this healing is bringing about.

A child suffering from asthma might be treated in this manner : *" God is healing you. The hindrances against the full expression of His perfect health in you are giving way. His power is coming to you in greater fullness so that you may breathe more and more easily, deeply, fully; filling your lungs with health-giving air. Health is coming back to your lungs and bronchial passages, and soon God's will for health will be realised in you and you will be perfectly well."* On the completion of these suggestions the mother should withdraw without awaking the child.

As soon as a child has learnt to speak, it should be taught and encouraged to make its own suggestions, both night and morning. A simple Christian formula which might well serve the purpose is this :

> *Jesus makes me, day by day,*
> *A better boy (or girl), in every way.*

This is simple and rhythmical, and possesses the advantage of a rhyme. Or one might prefer :

> *God within me, day by day,*
> *Makes me better, in every way.*

Meanwhile the child's daily prayers should be cast in the autosuggestion form proposed above. That is, they should end in affirmation and thanksgiving that the requests made are already being granted.[1]

The application of Christian autosuggestion to the training of the child offers us a means, a highly potent means, of consecrating the little one to the service of

[1] In the matter of the removal of pain we do not recommend any departure, in the treatment of children, from the method advised by M. Coué. For details see *Practice of Autosuggestion,* chaps. ix and x.

God. We read frequently in the Bible of children being given to God, being consecrated to His use through a life of service in the Temple. But is it not obvious that the advent of the Kingdom can only be achieved when we are all consecrated to this end? Our consecration will not consist in assuming the office of priesthood. We cannot all be priests. There must be scholars as well as teachers. It will consist of an inward devotion, by which we become fit channels for the manifestation of God's love and power.

Whatever view we take of the nature of baptism we must admit, as a matter of common experience, that it does not secure, as it should ideally do, the conformity of the human will to the will of God. Any other means, more concrete and definite, which works toward the same end, must, if God's will is our sincere desire, be fully utilised. We submit that Christian autosuggestion is such a means; that, now the knowledge of it is made available for us, we have a moral obligation to make use of it. However effective it may be in the hands of the adult, its full power will only be manifested when it is allowed to influence the life from earliest childhood.

Finally, we would repeat the warning already offered in the foregoing. Our Christian suggestions to the child must be in the most general terms. Who are we to know the mind of God for another life, and to interpret it in living clay? Our aim must be to open and make clear the channel by which God Himself can act, and leave this divine action unobstructed by our own human misconceptions. Health, sanity, goodness, the manifestation of God in human life; these are the aims which should inspire all Christian autosuggestion for children.

CHAPTER XVI

PAIN

Neither shall there be any more pain.—Rev. xxi. 4.

A HEALTHY physical existence appears to be one in which we are scarcely conscious of possessing bodies at all. The body serves us best when it obeys all the behests of the mind without obtruding itself upon our notice. Then we are delightfully unaware either of health or unhealth: we have the simple joy of living. But the evolutionary process has gone further. It has made us capable of physical pleasures of all degrees of intensity, and these pleasures add colour and variety to life, so that when they do not naturally befall us we are tempted to seek them in artificial ways.

But this very sensibility to pleasure exposes us, in the nature of the case, to its opposite—pain. If physical pleasure in its natural incidence is an indication of fullness of life, physical pain denotes with equal clearness some retardation of life; it shows that the organism is not functioning as it should. The evil is due to imperfections in the evolved body, which has not yet evolved far enough, or to ignorant treatment of the body, or to accident, or to wrongdoing and sin—either of the sufferer or of the race. In any case the pain is a signal that something is amiss, and that our attention is required to set it right. Such a signal is obviously of great value: there can be no question of suppressing it unless we can substitute for it something equally

144

effective and less unpleasant. The evil of pain lies not in its existence, but in its persistence when its work is done. Just as we should object to a fog-signal which emitted a continual roar from the first incidence of the fog until its final dispersal, so we legitimately object to a pain which keeps us in a state of anguish long after we have taken all precautions to remove its cause.

Here, however, we must pause to meet an objection, viz., that pain and suffering are an aid to saintliness, and therefore, if not actually sought for, should not be actively assailed.

Now, it is a truism that misery of any kind is capable of bringing to light virtues hitherto hidden and unrealised. A starving mother may show a holy unselfishness which in prosperity she would have no occasion to exercise. War, famine, pestilence, fire and flood, all afford opportunities for heroic and selfless courage, but for this reason to encourage and foster such disasters would be impious and insane. The fact that God is able to produce beauty and splendour out of suffering is a tribute to His wisdom, a sign of the vastness of His strength. But it is in *overcoming* these barriers that His wisdom and strength are manifested, not in passively submitting to them. We must admit, too, that God does not always succeed in overcoming them. Hampered by His refusal to coerce our wills, He frequently fails to smelt the gold from the ore in the fire of suffering. Although in some natures disaster breeds strength, it produces in a larger number fear and despair. For one man whom the fire tempers there are many it consumes. For one hero of the battlefield there are some dead, many maimed, and still more who are shocked out of health and sanity.

This is equally the case with physical pain. If here and there pain produces a saint, it far more often produces selfishness. The afflicted are often crabbed, peevish and cruel. The world is right in admiring health and vigour, and in expecting virtue from their possessors.

It is our duty to enlist in the divine crusade for overcoming evil in all its forms, and we must be thankful for a new weapon with which to drive out persistent physical pain. We submit that the overcoming of pain is a means of doing the will of God; that the religious objections offered against it are fallacious.[1] But there remain certain medical objections.

Pain, as we have already seen, is a signal, which informs the consciousness that there is something amiss with the body. It is therefore argued that to remove pain is to run the risk of allowing some disease or disorder to develop without our being aware of it. If the aim of M. Coué's method were to render the body insensible to pain, this objection would undoubtedly stand. But it is not. M. Coué aims at removing pain *when it has delivered its message*. We remove this disagreeable signal *as soon as* it has done its work, just as we so arrange our telephones that the call-bell ceases to ring as soon as the receiver is lifted. Why should we allow pain to continue for hours, even for days or weeks, when we and our medical advisers have heard its message and taken all possible steps to set things right? M. Coué teaches us that if we experience pain we should immediately proceed to get rid of

[1] When Sir James Simpson began to make use of chloroform in obstetric surgery he was bitterly reproached for doing away with God-sent suffering. The quotation of Genesis ii. 21 vindicated him: " And the Lord God caused a deep sleep to fall upon Adam."

it, but we should also proceed to get rid of its cause, both by the aid of the physician and by autosuggestion, for the two should work together.

There are many pains, however, that teach us nothing. If I burn my hand I am quite sufficiently aware of the wound, and do not need to suffer intense and continued pain in order to make me apply ointment and bandages. Nature's safeguard is present in crude excess. Indeed, it becomes a positive hindrance, for recent experiments have proved that pain is a direct obstacle to healing.[1] Apart from physical effects, it is obvious that the disintegrating effect of pain upon the mind is destructive of that calm confidence and faith which are such a powerful aid to recovery. It should be mentioned, too, that in M. Coué's opinion the procedure for removing pain acts not only on the pain itself, but on its cause; in getting rid of the pain, it does something also to get rid of the cause of the pain. This, however, is a point on which further investigation is needed, though M. Coué's contention seems a reasonable one, and is based on direct observation.

There is one further objection. Through the coming of pain I become aware of some internal disorder. I remove the pain by autosuggestion, and the disorder is treated by medical means and by my own suggestions. Suppose, however, that for some reason the disorder is aggravated. An intensification of the pain should give me warning of this, and so enable me to secure a modification of the treatment. But since I have removed my pain, this intensification cannot take place, and I remain without the needful warning. It is, of course, unlikely that a malady which made its presence

[1] See Dr. J. A. Hadfield: *Immortality*, article "The Mind and the Brain," p. 52.

felt by means of pain would become aggravated without a renewal, at least sufficient to be sensible, of the pain which is its natural symptom. But to give the objection its full force we will assume that this is so. I have so completely removed the pain that even when the malady is aggravated I receive no warning by means of pain.

The mere recognition of such an eventuality places us in a position to preclude it. After removing the pain in the initial instance nothing more is necessary than to suggest that it will not recur *unless* the morbid condition which occasioned it should be augmented; if for any reason we should grow worse, the renewal of the pain will at once apprise us of the fact.

However valuable pain may be, no one is likely to dispute its extreme unpleasantness. It performs its function in a most objectionable manner. If I wish to inform the occupants of the house next door to mine that a member of their family has been run over in the street, I do not attract their attention by throwing stones at the windows or setting fire to the house. My message will give them sufficient trouble without so graceless and damaging a method of delivery. But pain informs us of our physical misfortunes by an analogous proceeding. Any method by which the news could be broken more graciously would do much to make life happier.

Now, autosuggestion may quite possibly provide such a method. In the treatment of patients suffering from fits, M. Coué employs the following technique: he suggests that the patient will be aware of the approaching paroxysm some time in advance, and so will be in a position, by a timely use of suggestion, to avert the fit altogether. Here we find a state of mental

awareness doing the work which is commonly performed by pain—acting as a signal that all is not well
with us.   There seems no logical reason why such a
method should not be extended to further cases; pain
being supplanted by an intuition, a state of mental
awareness, furnished by the Unconscious.   Or, if a
purely mental indication should prove difficult or un-
desirable, we might succeed in substituting for physical
pain a sensation, which, though imperious, is not pain-
ful.   Certain of our functions already work by such
an arrangement.

Pain is not only a grim and churlish messenger: it
is also an unreliable one.   A man may be attacked by
mortal disease without suffering a twinge of discom-
fort, while the decay of a tooth will cause hardly bear-
able suffering.   In attempting to control pain we
should not lose sight of this fact.   If a substitute can
be found for pain it should be one which will inform
us of the incidence of those deep-seated ills which the
pain-signal at present ignores.

M. Coué's method of combating pain is new to
mental therapeutics.   As is well known, it consists of
the rapid repetition of the phrase *ça passe* (going), accompanied by a gentle stroking of the seat of the pain.
The necessary characteristic of this phrase is that it
should allow itself to be rapidly repeated.   It is obvious
that any addition would render it more difficult to
articulate, and so retard the speed of its repetition.
There is therefore a practical difficulty in the way of
incorporating in it an explicit acknowledgment of
God's help.   But is such continual acknowledgment
necessary?   The attempt consciously to relate every
activity to God is apt to result in external show, in
the repetition of vain unreverent phrases.   Truly we

give thanks before meat—or some of us do—but none of us attempts to give thanks before each mouthful! The best means of relating the removal of pain to God, who is the source of our power, would seem to be by a word of prayer before the practice begins. Before beginning the repetition one might give a moment to this thought: " *God does not mean this pain to persist, and by His power I shall now remove it.*"

When pain is intense and prolonged, there is a great advantage in obtaining someone to make the suggestions for us.

This method of removing pain merely seeks to do by mental and spiritual means what the medical profession does by the administration of anæsthetics and drugs. But the use of such remedies requires the greatest caution. Under medical guidance they may be used, of course, with perfect safety, but when expert advice is lacking, their misuse may lead to serious evils. The normal dose soon fails of its effect, and the temptation comes to increase it, often with perilous consequences, both physical and moral. The removal of pain by the method of autosuggestion is not open to these objections.

It is also in line with our Saviour's practice as a physician. He never scrupled to remove disease and pain. It is not recorded that He said to any sufferer: " Your pain has a moral value; it is making you more saintly, and therefore I will not remove it." On the contrary, in instance after instance, we are told, " He healed them all." True, before He was nailed to the cross He refused the anodyne offered Him,[1] and it has been conjectured that the endurance of acute physical pain was essential for the value of His sacrifice. But

[1] St. Matt. xxvii. 34.

is this so? In the Temple sacrifices no value was at-
tached to the suffering of the animals: they were put
to death in the speediest possible manner. It was the
life, offered through death, and symbolised by the
blood, that constituted the atoning efficacy of the sacrifice. May we not reverently conjecture that our Lord
refused the medicated wine because He did not need it?

CHAPTER XVII

SOME OBJECTIONS

I acknowledge a perfect man to be in Christ: not the body of a man only, not, with the body, a sensitive soul without a rational, but very man.

St. Augustine, *Confessions.*

While we hope that the arguments and proposals contained in this little book will be vigorously tested and criticised, we see no reason why certain misconceptions which are almost sure to arise should not be dealt with in advance.

One of the most serious and fundamental of these is the idea that the Christian use of autosuggestion is something approaching an " exploitation " of God.

Mr. Clutton Brock in his two books (*Studies in Christianity* and *What is the Kingdom of Heaven?*) rightly points out that as long as we regard the universe as a means of satisfying our egotistical demands and requirements we are infallibly cut off from its beauty and its spiritual significance; we misunderstand it as completely as a person who listens to a symphony of Beethoven, expecting it to give some information of use to himself, " information that will help him to increase his income or cure his indigestion." We can only understand and appreciate the universe by entering into a relation of *love* towards it, and not one of *use.* Much more, then, must our relation towards God be one of love and surrender rather than a desire to use His gifts for our own selfish ends.

But to the religious mind all the laws of Nature are a manifestation of God's power and God's order, and therefore we are compelled by the mere fact of living to make use of God at every moment. God, in this sense, drives our steam-engines, even explodes our bombs, and directs the flight of torpedoes. To say that we must not make use of God is to say that we must not exist at all. God allows Himself freely to be made use of; indeed, He compels us to make use of Him. Nevertheless, the distinction is a real and valuable one. In our personal and direct relationship with God, which takes place through prayer, there is all the difference in the world between the mental attitude which demands the means of satisfying its own desires and that which loses all thought of self in the loving contemplation of God's beauty and perfection. If Christian autosuggestion were a mere technique by which we could exploit God's power for low ends, we should lose by it more than we could gain. That it is possible so to use it we do not deny. There is nothing good which cannot be abused. The freedom of choice with which God has endowed us entails, as a necessary consequence, the ability to abuse and degrade His gifts. But we submit that no one but a moral pervert—a very rare type—would set out consciously and of set purpose to use this power for the ends of evil.

The thought of submitting to God's will is repugnant to many people because they have a false conception of the nature of God's will—a conception directly attributable to mistaken religious teaching. God's will has been represented as the repression of innocent desires for happiness and joy. To God has been attributed the malicious plan of " filling the world with temptations and saving only those who refuse all natural joys." [1] But when we accept Christ's teaching we realise the falsity of such conceptions. God is our loving Father, whose will for us is health, joy and the fullest, completest life. Our self-life is a parody, a foolish caricature, of the splendid fullness of joy and power which God intends for us. Who then would hesitate to take the will of God as his own completest good?

The method of Christian autosuggestion contains effective safeguards against its degradation to merely selfish ends. It requires the sloughing off of our personal will, to make way for God's will. It requires us to repeat a general formula which makes goodness, in the widest sense, the aim of our practice, and leaves the Indwelling Spirit to choose the channels by which this goodness shall be made manifest. We present our lives to God to shape and determine them according to His will. Even where we ask of God specific benefits we have to be sure, so far as we humanly can be, that they are in accordance with His wishes for us, and where we are doubtful as to the nature of His will, we seek by Christian autosuggestion to discover it. The essence of Christian autosuggestion is not making use of God, but allowing God to make use of us.

But we must beware of that exaggerated particularity which so fears to act otherwise than in accordance with God's will that it never acts at all. Here again faith is needful. When we have asked God to show us His will and received enlightenment we must proceed to act boldly. God cannot use a sluggish and stationary mind. No doubt in the practice of Christian autosuggestion there are innumerable loopholes by which error may enter, but they are vastly outnum-

[1] *What is the Kingdom of Heaven?* p. 45.

bered by the channels of truth. The field of our hearts
will not thus be entirely denuded of tares, but at least
we shall nurture the wheat.

We foresee also that the manner in which we have
interpreted the miracles of Christ may bring on us the
serious reproach that we have taken away His Divinity
and reduced Him to a mere man.

In reply to this we can only say that it is of the
essence of the Christian Faith that Jesus Christ was
truly man—the Son of God become man. Not man
in the sense merely of possessing a man's body of flesh
and blood, but also of having a true human mind and
will, and the full range of human emotions—in other
words, a human soul. Anything short of this would
make Him only partially man. It was as man that He
determined to live on earth, and His miracles were
wrought not in virtue of His inherent Godhead, but
by His faith in the Father and by requesting and using
the Father's power. He stated this Himself and
showed it in His *modus operandi.* We here trench on
some of the deepest mysteries of our Faith, but it is
sufficient for our purpose to say that while Jesus Christ
is the Eternal Son of God, He surrendered the consciousness and exercise of His divine nature that He
might live on earth the life of man, only without the
stain and disablement of sin. His miracles were not
something akin to magic or sorcery: Christ was not a
conjuror, amazing the ignorant rustics of Palestine
with exhibitions of His dexterity. His miracles were
examples of the mighty power of faith, and He required His disciples to go and do likewise.

The argument that in healing the sick Christ made
use of the power of suggestion which exists in every
human mind, does not militate against His inherent

deity any more than does the fact that Christ hungered and wept, was weary and marvelled, used reason and persuasion. And we may fortify our position by quoting from Professor A. G. Hogg's remarkable book, *Redemption from this World.* No one can doubt this original thinker's belief in our Lord's Godhead, yet this is what he says: "The miracles of Jesus were acts of faith, and by our Lord Himself His own miracle-working was regarded not as the exercise of a personally inherent divine attribute or prerogative, but as a feature of His human Messianic vocation. To accept such a view of the matter involves no disloyalty to our Lord, nor any departure from our Christian estimate of His Person. It is forced upon us by His own words and attitude. Even in His miracle-working He was very Man" (p. 65). And again: "Nowhere does He represent His miracles as the exercise of an incommunicable divine prerogative. He performs them as One commissioned thereto by His Heavenly Father; He speaks of them as being wrought at His instance by the Spirit of God" (p. 67). We might quote further from this book and from other books by outstanding orthodox divines, but we have written enough to dispose of the reproach that we have in any way diminished the majesty and sublimity of Christ.[1]

It is sometimes strangely argued that autosuggestion destroys faith. By this is meant, we suppose, that faith in God is supplanted by faith in the powers of one's own mind. But faith in one's own mind *is* faith in God, for the mind is an instrument fashioned by God and filled with the energy God supplies. Autosugges-

[1] See on this subject: Sanday, *Christologies* (1910); Weston, *The One Christ;* Forsyth, *The Person and Place of Jesus Christ;* Gore, *Belief in Christ* (1922), chap. vii.

tion, as we have shown in the preceding chapters, so far from destroying faith, is itself faith in action.

This charge of destroying faith is not a new accusation. It is always the timid outcry of traditional religionism that suspects anything new, and is afraid to face indubitable facts. Unhappily for itself, organised Christian religion has brought the same charge against the greatest discoveries in the history of science; it has feared that a belief in this or that would upset the balance of true religion and diminish the majesty of the Eternal God. And in almost every case, after a period of bigoted and uncomprehending obstruction, it has been forced to admit the offending idea into the dogmatic enclosure and has found itself thereby enriched and empowered.

Although in some of the criticisms passed on M. Coué and his methods by religious writers one cannot but feel, as Mr. Orlo Williams says,[1] "a kind of jealousy," the attitude of many of the most authoritative leaders of the Christian Churches is distinctly favourable and sympathetic. Some, like Dr. R. F. Horton, Mr. H. C. Carter,[2] Mr. Pym, and the Dean of Chester,[3] warmly welcome autosuggestion as a valuable ally, and others, we feel sure, will come to take up the same position.

We claim that the practice of autosuggestion on the lines laid down by M. Coué and his expositor, Professor Charles Baudouin, has a greater significance for the Christian than for the secularist. It brings back to

[1] *Some Reflections on Autosuggestion,* by Orlo Williams, p. 15.
[2] *Autosuggestion and Religion,* by. H. C. Carter, M.A.
[3] The Dean of Chester's *M. Coué and his Gospel of Health* deals with many of the subjects discussed in these pages. Unfortunately it came into our hands only when this book was already in proof.

us after centuries of disuse the element of healing power which distinguished Christ's ministry and that of His apostles. It illuminates the meaning of prayer and faith, and settles the ancient controversy between faith and works. Finally, it offers a means by which the Church can escape from its present lethargy and impotence to become once more a source of energy, inspiration, and heroic life.

CPSIA information can be obtained at www.ICGtesting.com
Printed in the USA
BVOW041626180712

295527BV00003BA/191/A

9 781425 421670